True History of Some Of the Pioneers of Colorado

By
Luella Shaw

A REPRINT BY
WESTERN REFLECTIONS PUBLISHING COMPANY
LAKE CITY, COLORADO

A Reprint Published by
Western Reflections Publishing Company
P.O. Box 1149
951 N. Highway 149
Lake City, Colorado 81235

www.westernreflectionspub.com
westref@montrose.net

Copyright Western Reflections Publishing Company 2008
All rights reserved including the rights to reproduction in
whole or in part.

Printed in the United States of America

Library of Congress Number 2008924032

ISBN 978-1-932738-63-6

PROLOGUE

In *True History of Some of the Pioneers of Colorado*, Luella Shaw provides readers with "firsthand" insight into the events and lives of those who called Colorado home in the second half of the Nineteenth Century. In personal narratives, early pioneers Watson S. Coburn, Alston Knox Shaw, and John Patterson shed light on the "massacre" at Sand Creek, Native Americans of the time, Jim Reynolds and his outlaw gang, and what it was like to experience life when the West was young.

Luella Shaw first came to my attention through Ruth and Marvin Gregory, Colorado historians who lived in the town of Ouray. Ruth's mother, Luella, was born in 1886, to Charles and Ellen Shaw. Luella's parents married in 1881 and lived in Animas City (now Durango), Colorado.

Luella's father, Charles, had come to Colorado with his father George W. Shaw in 1863. George's family was the first to establish a home in the vicinity of Pueblo, Colorado, and they also lived in Georgetown, Colorado. In 1876, the family moved to Parrott City, now a ghost town, but then located between present-day Mancos and Durango. Records show that George built Animas City's first house and helped to build its first church.

In 1895, Luella's family moved to Silverton, where her father worked as a packer and freighter. Luella went to school near Howardsville, Colorado, and graduated from Silverton High School. When her brother, Charles, developed heart problems that were aggravated by the high altitude, Luella, her brother, and their mother moved to the farming and fruit raising community of Hotchkiss, while her father remained in Silverton. Luella married in Hotchkiss, and Ruth (Gregory) was born there.

Luella's maternal grandfather was also an early pioneer of Colorado. George Mock came to the area in 1859 from Missouri during the initial Colorado gold rush and settled in Georgetown, Colorado. Luella also had two uncles who participated in the battle at Sand Creek, later called "The Sand Creek Massacre."

Most of the Shaw family, including Luella, returned to the Silverton-Eureka-Howardsville area; but considerable time was also spent in Hotchkiss. Because of its mild climate, Hotchkiss was and still is a favorite retirement community. It was in Hotchkiss that Luella came to know well the three pioneers whose stories and personal narratives are included in her book.

Much of what Luella writes about concerns the "Sand Creek Massacre," a U. S. Cavalry and Native American battle, which has been the topic of heated debate over the years. Most feel it was an unwarranted massacre of Native Americans, including women and children. Others claim that it was a necessary, strategic attack on hostile, marauding Indians, who had to be caught off guard to save American lives. Truth, as well as beauty, may well be in the eye of the beholder. The pioneers of this book (Watson S. Coburn, Alston Knox Shaw, and John Patterson) all participated in the battle and felt that their actions were justified. Forty-five years after the battle, Luella wrote that the book's "object will be to furnish a true history of the incidents of the early settlement of the West and especially Colorado."

The men's stories also tell of other early pioneers and their hardships, Native Americans who they knew, and personal adventures; but the focus of the book is Luella's attempt to set the record straight about what happened at Sand Creek.

Western Reflections Publishing Company is proud to reprint this work, which has become exceedingly rare. By doing so, it is hoped that these stories will be made available to everyone who wants to know the way things "really were" – as recounted by these true pioneer settlers of Colorado.

P. David Smith

Publisher

MISS LUELLA SHAW

True History of Some of the Pioneers of Colorado

LUELLA SHAW

1909
PUBLISHED BY
W. S. COBURN, JOHN PATTERSON and A. K. SHAW
HOTCHKISS, COLORADO

COPYRIGHT 1909
BY
LUELLA SHAW

DENVER, COLO.
PRESS OF CARSON-HARPER CO.

Contents

	Page
PREFACE	7
CHAPTER I.—The Cause of the Combination of the Three Tribes Against the Whites. As told by W. S. Coburn	9
CHAPTER II.—Watson S. Coburn	15
CHAPTER III.—My First Trip Across the Plains. By W. S. Coburn	19
CHAPTER IV.—Raid Up the Platte. As told by W. S. Coburn	23
CHAPTER V.—Massacre of the Hungate Family	33
CHAPTER VI.—Jim Reynolds and His Gang	39
CHAPTER VII.—Alston Knox Shaw	49
CHAPTER VIII.—Proceedings of Company "A." As told by A. K. Shaw	53
CHAPTER IX.—John Patterson	67
CHAPTER X.—Proceedings of Company "C." By John Patterson	69
CHAPTER XI.—Est Pinosa, the Mexican Desperado	73
CHAPTER XII.—Sand Creek Fight. As told by Patterson and Shaw	79
CHAPTER XIII.—A Few Incidents During the Fight	87
CHAPTER XIV.—Cause of the Sand Creek Fight	99
CHAPTER XV.—Justice of the Fight	107
CHAPTER XVI.—Sand Creek a Decisive Battle	115
CHAPTER XVII.—The Yellow Haired Boy	121
CHAPTER XVIII.—March to Fort Larnard. By A. K. Shaw and John Patterson	127
CHAPTER XIX.—Shaw and the Horses	131

Page

CHAPTER XX.—Little Happenings in Denver............ 137
CHAPTER XXI.—Depredations of Indians on Geary's Neighbors. Told by J. Patterson................... 143
CHAPTER XXII.—Captain Peacock's Fight. As told by W. S. Coburn................................... 149
CHAPTER XXIII.—Indian Charley. By W. S. Coburn 151
CHAPTER XXIV.—Little Horse and His Band. As told by W. S. Coburn................................... 159
CHAPTER XXV.—Two Face. By W. S. Coburn.......... 167
CHAPTER XXVI.—Standing Elk......................... 173
CHAPTER XXVII.—Massacre at Fort Phil Kearney....... 179
CHAPTER XXVIII.—Mexican Peter Arrago. As told by W. S. Coburn................................... 181
CHAPTER XXIX.—A Few Minor Experiences. As told by W. S. Coburn................................... 187
CHAPTER XXX.—Red Bead, Roberts and the Comanches.. 197
CHAPTER XXXI.—Fight with Eagle Claw. By W. S. Coburn 201
CHAPTER XXXII.—Fight of General Forsyth. As told by A. K. Shaw..................................... 211
CHAPTER XXXIII.—A Trip Into Montana. As told by A. K. Shaw..................................... 217
CHAPTER XXXIV.—A Trip to the Missouri River. As told by A. K. Shaw............................. 227
CHAPTER XXXV.—A Buffalo Hunt. As told by John Patterson 233
CHAPTER XXXVI.—My First Introduction to Colorado. As told by Mrs. John Patterson.................. 237
CHAPTER XXXVII.—The Advent of the Union Pacific Railroad in the Summer and Fall of 1867. By W. S. Coburn 241
CHAPTER XXXVIII.—Gold Miners from Montana Returning to the States After a Successful Trip.......... 249
CHAPTER XXXIX.—Loyalty to the Pioneers............ 253
CHAPTER XL.—Conclusion 265

Come, you children of the pioneers,
    And join me in their praise;
Let us shout three rousing cheers,
    To awake the memory of their frays.
Our fathers, they came to the land
    Of redskins and buffalo,
And took a firm, steadfast stand,
    To rid the country of its foe.
Some were settlers, others were scouts,
    All aiming to build up the frontier
And run the redskins out,
    Who were scalping all, far and near.
They suffered privations and hardships,
    These strong-hearted men of the wild,
As they made their many trips
    Over the prairie, but not once defiled.
Though unseen dangers hovered near,
    On open plains or in mountains high,
They bravely pushed forward with a cheer,
    Determined to conquer the West or die.
When the Indian massacres were spreading,
    And the frontier was flooded with untold fears,
And all the settlers were dreading
    The oncoming blood-stained years,

Governor Evans realized the vast need
  Of defense and protection on the border;
So Colonel Chivington bravely took the lead,
  And marched his band out in perfect order.
Just a hand full of volunteers
  Marched out to defeat or victory.
One aim had these brave pioneers,
  'Twas to save this western country.
They did not march to fife and drum,
  In grand military array,
With bayonets flashing in the sun,
  Or waving colors bright and gay,
But valiantly kept step to the rhyme
  Of aching hearts and thoughts of those
That fell victims to the bloody crime
  Of the savages—the settlers' worst foe.
They marched 'neath the standard of right,
  These volunteers brave and true,
And fought with all their might
  To win a home, my friends, for you.
They chased those bloodthirsty red devils
  That had covered the West with blood and tears;
They ran them on the hills and levels,

Like the redskins had once done the pioneers.
Only a few of them now remain
    To see the outcome of their deeds;
The growth of their once barren plain
    That now supplies all our needs.
We owe to Chivington and his band
    A debt we can never repay,
For taking their brave, firm stand,
    Thus starting our West of today.
The West of grandeur and wealth,
    With its schools and enterprises,
The West of good cheer and health,
    And many other glad surprises.
Reverence to the memory of those years
    Of struggles and sorrows on the frontier—
Gratitude in our hearts for the Volunteers
    And our forefathers—the Pioneers.

PREFACE.

In presenting this narrative to the public, its object will be to furnish a true history of some of the incidents of the early settlement of the West, and especially of Colorado.

Being intimately acquainted with parties cognizant of the facts related, we feel certain of the literal truths of the statements contained in this book.

There have been so many publications put upon the market purporting to be true history of frontier life, that utterly fail to convey the faintest idea of the real facts, that this work is undertaken.

It is impossible for the rising generations to conceive but a remote idea of the privations and dangers from hostile Indians that the pioneers endured in the early settlement of the West. This work will give an insight into the lives of some of the early settlers who endured the hardships and privations that they underwent for the sake of paving the way to our present civilization, where towns, cities and railroads have sprung into existence as if by magic.

CHAPTER I.

THE CAUSE OF THE COMBINATION OF THE THREE TRIBES AGAINST THE WHITES.

As Told by W. S. Coburn.

After spending the last forty-five years on the frontier, beginning in the then Territory of Kansas, Nebraska, Colorado, Wyoming, Utah, Idaho, Nevada, New Mexico, Arizona and Montana, and being a close observer of cause and effect in passing events, it will, no doubt, be of interest to the general public to know the real cause of the uprising and consolidation of the three tribes of Indians, namely, the Sioux, Cheyennes and Arapahoes, against the whites.

The Sioux Nation was the most powerful and numerous of any of the tribe of Indians on the North American continent, at one time numbering one hundred and twenty thousand warriors and consisting of three distinct bands, called the Yankton Sioux, who inhabited the northern boundary of the United many of whom lived in Minnesota.

The Bruls Sioux held the territory of North and South Dakota, and the Ogalalie Sioux, who occupied the plains of Colorado.

In the fall of 1862, when the United States was engaged in the Civil war, Minnesota had been settling up pretty fast, and was crowding in on the territory of the Yankton Sioux, who were very friendly with the whites and often enjoyed the hospitality of the settlers in the small places and in the vicinity of New Ulm.

About this time they conceived the idea of stopping the white settlers from coming into that part of Minnesota. Knowing that the United States was plunged into the Civil War and, as they thought, fully occupied with their own domestic troubles, it would be the most opportune time for them to execute their plans.

Accordingly they held secret councils and matured their plans of attack and massacre without the least suspicion on the part of the frontier settlers, with whom they had been so friendly. One old squaw, however, knew of their plans and notified some of the white women who had been very kind to her and advised them to go to safety at once, but the whites did not believe the Indians would do them any harm and ignored the admonition of the old squaw; so accordingly on the night of September 23rd, 1862, (if my memory serves me right), the Indians, according to previous arrangement, raised, as if by one man, in all parts of the settlement, and began to burn buildings and kill men, women and children as fast as they could get to them. This massacre lasted a day and a night until some three hundred settlers were killed and their homes laid in ashes.

The United States troops were soon in pursuit and captured some three hundred Indians and took them to the military prison at Rock Island on the Mississippi river between Illinois and Iowa. There they held them until the spring of 1863, when they were tried by court-martial and twenty-three of the leaders were sentenced to be hung; they were duly executed and the balance were made to witness the hanging. The orders from the war department were for the soldiers to take the remaining Indians out on the plains and turn them loose, with instruction to never return to Minnesota.

At this time nearly all the Indians on the plains were at war with each other over disputed territory of their hunting grounds.

The Omahas and Winnebagoes were weak tribes without much ambition, and were satisfied to live and beg from the few settlers in the vicinity of Omaha.

The Pawnees were located on the Loop Fork of the South Platte river and were deadly enemies of the Sioux, the disputed territory being near old Fort Kearney, from there west for two hundred miles up the Platte, and from the line of New Mexico south for six hundred miles.

In the north, the Ogulalies had supreme control, only when menaced by the Pawnees on the east and the Cheyennes on the west, who claimed one hundred miles of the Platte river and some five hundred miles north and south from the west end of the Cheyennes' territory. They claimed about sixty miles along the base of the mountains, where Denver, Colorado Springs, Greeley and Pueblo now stand. Up in the mountains the Utes claimed their hunting grounds, but would occasionally go down and trespass on the Arapahoes' territory; then there was sure to be war when this was found out.

This was the condition when nearly three hundred of the murderous band of Yankton Sioux were turned loose on the plains among their kindred.

They at once told their friends, Ogulalies, what a terrible crime the whites had committed in hanging twenty-three of their comrades and chiefs. Hanging, by the way, is the most ignoble death for an Indian imaginable. This remnant of three hundred at once advocated consolidation with all the Indians with whom they were at home, to fight and exterminate the whites. They called councils of war with the Pawnees, who refused to listen.

They then made overtures to the Cheyennes and Arapahoes, when councils were held during the summer of 1863, and speeches made denouncing the whites and calling the Indians fools for fighting among themselves and killing each other, but to combine and annihilate the whites. These councils finally prevailed late in the fall, between the three tribes of Sioux, Cheyennes and Arapahoes. The Pawnees in the east and the Utes in the mountains to the west refusing to participate with their enemies.

This combined force of three tribes soon commenced their depredations, covering a territory five hundred miles wide, east and west of the northern line of New Mexico, to the Canadian line in the northward, a distance of some nine hundred miles.

Forts were established, and soldiers stationed all along the Arkansas and Platte rivers to stop their murderous and destroying raids. But the Indian war on the plains lasted about fifteen years before the government finally got them subdued.

During this time hundreds of emigrants and soldiers were killed and scalped, and millions of dollars worth of property destroyed and stolen.

A few years ago the government created an Indian Depredation Bureau and sent attorneys west to take evidence to establish the claims of those who had been raided. The narrator proved up on his claim for stock stolen and hay burnt to the amount of eighteen thousand, two hundred and eighty dollars and the attorney told him that there was upwards of seventy million dollars in claims for Indian depredations and the government was anxious to have them all filed and settled as soon as possible, since which time there has been no effort on the part of Congress to take the matter up and amend one article so the claimants can be settled with.

W. S. COBURN

CHAPTER II.

WATSON S. COBURN.

Watson S. Coburn was born on June 4, 1838, in Decatur, Massachusetts.

After living in the New England states about twenty-one years, he decided to go West. He made Chicago, then a town of a hundred and nine inhabitants, his first stop, where he remained six months, before going to Springfield, Illinois. While in Springfield the civil war broke out and he went to join the army. Failing to get in on account of the quorum being filled, each time he applied, he was given a position as a sutler to sell goods to the soldiers.

He was in the siege at Vicksburg, which lasted forty-seven days and nights, and when Pemberton was forced to surrender to Grant and the town was opened, Coburn was the first citizen to enter Vicksburg. He went in with the first regiment of soldiers on July 4, 1863.

About this time he quit the army and went into the commission business at Omaha, Nebraska. Six months afterwards his partner died, so he sold out and came to Colorado, since which time he has been all over the western states. He lived on his ranch, which was called the Chicago ranch and situated on the Platte river, during the years of 1865, 1866 and 1867.

When the Union Pacific Railroad was built from Julesburg on west in 1868, this put a stop to the overland freight and travel and consequently put the feed stations out of business. Mr. Coburn then went to work for the railroad, contracting for the fuel. He was the first man to build a house and dig a well in Cheyenne, Wyoming. Later he took a supply of goods and moved along ahead of the railroad and sold goods to the graders. When the track reached Promontory Point west of Ogden, Utah, on May 10, 1869, his store business was stopped. He went to the then new state of Kansas and began dealing in Texas cattle, which proved unsuccessful, so he returned to Colorado. Mr. Coburn's next venture was freighting and mining, and when the Ute Reservation was thrown open in 1882, he took up a ranch on the western slope, between the present towns of Paonia and Hotchkiss, Colorado. He started a commercial orchard on his ranch, and has since made his home there.

CHAPTER III.

MY FIRST TRIP ACROSS THE PLAINS.

By W. S. Coburn.

After several months in business in Omaha, Nebraska, my partner, Silas Reena, took sick with typhoid fever and died, and after closing and settling his estate, I determined to come west to Colorado.

Accordingly I rigged up a four-mule team and loaded with goods for Denver, accompanied by fifteen other teams.

When we arrived at Fort Kearney, about two hundred miles west of Omaha, we were notified by the officers at the fort that we could proceed no further until enough emigrants and freighters came along to make a party of one hundred well armed men and that we should have to organize and elect a captain whose orders would have to be obeyed for self protection against the hostile Indians, who were very numerous for the next four hundred miles. At the end of two days we had the required number and proceeded to elect a captain to take charge and much to my surprise and much against my protest, they elected me to this position. I argued and protested, having never had any experience with hostile Indians, but to no purpose, so I accepted and promised to do the best I could and we started the third morning with emigrants and freighters, including women and children with all kinds of dispositions. No one but those who have had experience with such a conglomerate mass of humanity can realize the anxiety and trials to keep them all satisfied, and in spite of my best efforts misunderstandings would arise.

In one day's drive we passed the remnants of what would have been eleven wagons, loaded with a stamp mill for Central City, Colorado, that had been burned, the men scalped and killed and the oxen driven away. This had a tendency to keep the rear teams well closed up.

This was in July and the weather was quite warm in the middle of the day and for this reason it was necessary to start early in the morning and camp for a few hours in the heat of the day. This starting at daylight caused much inconvenience among the families of women and children and some of the men.

However, we were making good time and had seen no Indians until we got about forty miles west of Fort Sedgwick, when we camped one night just before crossing some sand hills. Our crowd had begun to think that we were comparatively safe from the Indians and the next morning some of the families were slow in getting ready to start, and one team loaded with dry goods and owned by two men by the names of Auery and Smith came to me and asked permission to pull over the sand hills before it got too hot, saying they would take all chances of seeing Indians. I reluctantly consented. They were about one-half mile ahead of the train when Mr. Auery missed his meerschaum pipe and stopped and turned to search for it in the wagon. Smith got off the wagon and said he would walk on ahead. While Auery was back in the covered wagon he heard a war whoop, and he looked out and saw twelve Indians ride from behind the sand hill and surround Smith, scalp and kill him just two hundred and twelve feet from the wagon. Auery thought his time had come, but when all the Indians dismounted and began to yell and dance around the body of Smith, he quickly slid off the wagon, dropped the tugs, mounted one of the horses, and came dashing back to the train. When the train got to the place of the killing, the Indians, after looting the wagon, had mounted their ponies and went flying over the prairie with whole bolts of calico and red flannel streaming behind them in the wind.

We wrapped poor Smith's body up in a blanket and buried him near where he fell. We were then a hundred and sixty miles from Denver, where we arrived safe and sound on the seventh day of August, 1865.

CHAPTER IV.

RAID UP THE PLATTE.

As Told by W. S. Coburn.

As we came over the road to Denver, we noticed many ruins of what had been feed stations. This was caused by a general attack on every ranch from Fort Morgan to Fort Sedgwick, a distance of one hundred miles, by from two hundred and fifty to five hundred Indians to each ranch. The attack occurred on the morning of the fourteenth day of January, 1865.

These feed ranches or stations were situated about twelve miles apart, a half day's travel, to accommodate the overland travel with such supplies they often ran short of.

Every ranch, together with its stables and hay stacks, was burned to the ground, except one owned and occupied by Old Man Godfrey, ever afterward known as Old Fort Wicked.

Many people were scalped and killed, but the most complete annihilation at any one place was at the American Ranch, where Mr. Morris and five hired men were killed and his wife and two children (aged, respectively, eight months and a boy four years) were taken prisoners and made to ride bare back in their retreat and suffer all other kinds of indignities of these red devils in human forms. At the end of two days' travel, when they were out of reach of pursuers, Old Two Face, a Cheyenne chief, who claimed Mrs. Morris for his captive, came to her and took the baby out of her arms, and naturally the child cried and wanted back to its mother, and when he tried to quiet it without success, he became enraged and took it by one foot and one arm and raised it as high as he could above his head and threw it to the ground with all his strength, then jumped on it, crushing its chest and ribs and then walked away. The mother took the child and did all she could to save it. In about two hours Two Face (who will be referred to later when he gets what is coming to him), returned and after seeing how near dead the child was, ordered her to go out on a sand hill near the camp and dig a hole with her hands and bury the baby. She vigorously refused to, so the chief then pointed to the sun and indicated by his hand that when the sun had moved a certain distance, indicating about one hour, he would return and if she had not obeyed his orders he would scalp her. Several squaws sympathized with her and offered to help her, knowing that Two Face would kill her if she failed to comply. Accordingly she went and dug the little grave, with the help of the squaws, and wrapped up the little form and buried it with her own hands, while it was yet alive. The little boy was traded off to another tribe and the mother never saw him again. After this great raid the Indians scattered in small bands, when out of reach of any soldiers.

Two Face, who had Mrs. Morris, went north and about three months afterwards appeared at Fort Benton, Montana, under a flag of truce and proposed to sell the white squaw to the commander of the post. The officer at once commenced negotiations, and after giving him a large amount of flour, tobacco, bacon and some trinkets, Two Face brought Mrs. Morris in and surrendered her and was allowed to depart as he had entered, under a white rag tied on a stick, called the flag of truce. The officers at once furnished her some money and transportation on a boat bound for St. Louis. When she arrived safely she wrote back all the particulars of her capture, long stay and abuse with the Indians.

We will now refer to the time when the attack was made on the American Ranch. All the men and family were in the room back of the one where all the goods were kept. Mr. Morris was playing a fiddle when suddenly Mrs. Morris heard a noise in the front part and at once called Mr. Morris' attention to it. On opening the door he saw the room was full of Indians, who immediately gave the war whoop and tried to kill him. He then opened fire with his revolver and killed three of them before they could get out of the door. After barricading the door the men were able to hold their own until the latter part of the day when the Indians set fire to the stables and a large quantity of hay adjoining the house. The smoke poured into the house in such volumes that the inmates were about to suffocate. Seeing that it would be impossible to stand it much longer, Mr. Morris took half a bottle of strychnine that he kept to poison wolves with, and divided it into two decanters of whiskey behind the counter, after shaking it up; he told his wife to take the children and go out to the front door and give herself up, while he and the men would try to escape out the back way. It was a well known fact that the Indians seldom killed a white woman, hence the plan taken. The men, however, were all killed and scalped a short distance from the house.

Just before the attack, two men, Gus Hall and one called Big Steve (half or two-thirds of the transient men at the ranches were known only by nick names) left the ranch with ox teams and started to the cedar canons, sixteen miles away, to get a load of wood. About nine o'clock in the morning, soon after the fight commenced, the Indians discovered these two men, where they had crossed the river on the ice and eleven Indians went over to get their scalps. Nine of the Indians made an attack in front while two of them took positions on the ice under the bank below and above the two men. Here they maintained a cross fire. After several hours Big Steve was killed by the cross fire. Soon afterwards Gus

Hall was shot in the right leg, breaking it between the knee and ankle.

It was getting late in the day and the farm house was burned, the women and children taken prisoners and the men killed, all right in plain sight of Hall, who was unable to render any assistance.

Hall had not seen the Indians on the river for some time and as he noticed the ones at the ranch preparing to leave, he decided to raise up and look over the bank and see what had become of the Indians that had attacked him. He had already made up his mind that they would soon get him anyway, for he could not protect himself and there was no white person for miles around, and Indians lurking everywhere. As he raised up on one leg and carefully leaned over the bank another object was just as cautiously raising a bow and arrow and aiming from under the bank. When Hall peeped over the bank, an arrow shot up and passed clear through his chest and slid twenty-two feet on the ice back of him. Hall said he fell backwards and the Indian leaped up the bank with knife in his hands ready to scalp him when he raised his revolver and shot the Indian, who fell dead over on him. The rest seeing the others leave the ranch pulled out and left.

Gus Hall, with one leg broken and pierced through and through, night coming on and the ranch laid in ruins and his friends killed, was left in an almost helpless condition. He thought the Wisconsin Ranch, fourteen miles down the road, might possibly be all right, and decided to try to get to it, so he commenced his journey, on his hands and knees, crawling down the ice. Arriving at the ranch, after a journey lasting seventeen hours, he found it in ruins and everybody gone. The sod walls were warm and the ground covered with a foot or two of grain and flour that was also warm. Hall made up his mind that he would die that night, and crawled in on the warm grain where he was sheltered from the wind by the sod walls and soon became unconscious. A train of wagons with about a hundred men was making its way down to Omaha. As it passed these ranches the men would investigate the ruins to see how many had been killed and to bury the ones they found dead. While one of the party was looking around he discovered Hall curled up in a corner and holloed to the rest, "Here is a dead man." This aroused Hall and he said, "I am not dead yet, but I think I will be before long."

They carried him out and put him in a wagon and cared for him the best they could. They took him on to Omaha, hauling him four hundred miles. When they arrived at Omaha the doctors amputated his leg and cared for the wound caused by the arrow. In six months' time he got a cork leg and foot and came back to my place.

Mr. Godfrey's ranch, known all over the western country as Old Fort Wicked, was the only ranch that was not either partially or totally destroyed by this raid.

Godfrey had his place well fortified and as fast as Mrs. Godfrey ran the balls, he would call to his daughter, "Hurry up, Celia; more balls, Celia." As fast as Celia carried the bullets to him, he would fire at the Indians, and at every shot he would use an oath and say, "Take that, will you?" Nearly every shot took effect, and with another oath he would say, "There goes another." The Indians, getting more than they bargained for, as Godfrey would state it, soon went on to the next ranch.

They succeeded in burning the hay stacks and sheds at the Beaver ranch, but the inmates saved themselves by using the sod walls as fortifications.

At the next ranch the Murray brothers had six hundred head of cattle shot down and left lying on the flat; the hay and barns were burned, but the men escaped.

CHAPTER V.

MASSACRE OF THE HUNGATE FAMILY.

In June, 1863, just before the call for volunteers to subdue the Indians, Isaac P. Vanwomer had his cattle and horses on the range in the Coal creek country.

Hungate, with his family and five hired men, were living at the Vanwomer camp, as Hungate was looking after the cattle and horses.

About four o'clock one afternoon, Hungate and his men were on the west side of the creek when the Indians attacked the cabin. Knowing that his wife and children were in the cabin alone, Mr. Hungate hurried across to their aid, but was too late, as the Indians had already murdered them. He then tried to make his escape, but had only gone a few miles before the Indians overtook him. His companion stood on the opposite bank of the creek and witnessed the scene. Realizing that he could do nothing to help his friend, he hurried into Denver with the news of the uprising.

After riding forty-five miles, with dangers on every side, and expecting to fall into the hands of the dreaded redskins at any moment, he finally arrived at Vanwomer's home a little after midnight.

The report was not a surprise to the citizens of Denver, as there had been so much trouble with the Indians.

It did not take long for these brave, stout-hearted and strong frontiersmen to get ready for a start towards the camp, where they hoped to trail the Indians and rescue their friend and avenge the terrible death of his wife and children.

About noon that day, sixty-four heavily armed and well-mounted men bid their families and friends good-bye and turned onto the trail leading to the scene of the massacre. It took a great deal of courage to start on such a mission, for these men of the plains, being familiar with the treacherous habits of the Indians, knew that when they ventured out on such an undertaking they were in great danger, not only from exposure and hunger, but captivity by the Indians, which meant suffering and torture, eventually ending in death.

It was the knowledge of the terrible agony a captive must suffer at the hands of the bloodthirsty savages, that urged the unselfish and never-fearing pioneers to forget their danger and hurry to the rescue of Hungate.

After traveling all that afternoon and far into the night, some on account of exhaustion, or horses giving out on them, and for different reasons, one by one they were compelled to turn back. When at last, worn out, they decided to camp for the night, only four were left to go on with the work. Three of these were Alston Shaw, Dave Armstrong and Isaac Vanwomer. We are unable to learn the name of the fourth one.

Despite the many dangers surrounding them, they made camp just two hundred yards from where the Hungate cabin had stood. After a hasty breakfast, early the next morning, these four men began to investigate the horrible massacre. They found the bedding all torn up and the feathers from the bed ticks scattered all over the yard; the cabin was burned to the ground; a few feet away they found the body of Mrs. Hungate; it was lying with face downward and her throat cut from ear to ear. In one arm she was holding the body of her little girl, whose throat was also cut. Clasped in the other arm was her little boy with his throat cut and scalped as well. Their bodies were placed in a conveyance, brought for the purpose, to take the dead back to Denver for burial.

Vanwomer, Shaw, Armstrong and their companion went on to trail the Indians. They soon found thirty head of horses that had been stolen from Vanwomer's camp.

Hungate's saddle horse was shod, so by noticing the tracks, it did not take long to get onto his trail and also made it easy for them to follow it. After going about two miles from where the cabin stood, Shaw found Hungate's cowquirt. The stalk was all bloody, which indicated a struggle, so they were prepared for the worst.

A mile or two from where the quirt was found they came upon his body. Such a sight! No wonder these strong men were unnerved, for lying before them, stretched on the ground, horribly cut up, was their old friend Hungate. He had an arrow in each breast, his heart cut out, scalped, his throat cut and otherwise greatly mutilated and the wounds all fly blown.

The body was sent into Denver and buried by the side of his wife and children.

Vanwomer, Shaw and Armstrong continued their search for the horses. After looking several days without success they returned to Denver, none the worse for their adventure.

A band of Indians raided up the Fountain river, followed up Monument creek over the divide, stealing horses or whatever they could get their hands on. On Monument creek they took about sixty head of horses from Teachout. At the foot of the divide on the south side, they stole a number of McShane's horses; crossing the divide and going down on the head of Plum creek, they stole a large bunch of horses from Wakeman and his two sons, Mose and Wash. Then they headed for Cherry creek.

Henry Teachout raised a band of fifteen or twenty men in Colorado Springs and started in pursuit. They trailed the Indians over on to the Bijou Creek, but were unable to recover any of their horses.

CHAPTER VI.

JIM REYNOLDS AND HIS GANG.

Jim Reynolds was a miner working at California Gulch, now Leadville. He got permission from the governor of Colorado to go down into Texas, his native state, and raise a regiment for the Union army. When he started for Texas, people believed that he was honest in his object, but on his return they soon learned that his undertaking was not to aid the government, but to take advantage of it during its struggles and help himself.

He left Texas with twenty-two men, but only had eight men and nine first-class horses with him on the Platte.

The following narrative is only one of their numerous deeds. Nearly all of their attacks on the stage coaches were along the old Powell road. This road wound around through timber and over hills, down on the Platte again. Being a well-concealed road, it afforded shelter along the sides of it for the outlaws to hide in so they could not be seen until they would spring out on their victims.

This stage line was owned by Billy Berry, Ad Williamson and Bob Spotswood. They ran the stage from Denver by Breckenridge, Fairplay, Alma and back into Denver.

On one occasion, Reynolds and his gang held up the coach and robbed it of eighteen thousand dollars in gold dust, the United States mail and express. Among the passengers was a young girl who had been working in the hotel at Fairplay and saved up four hundred dollars of her own money and had the same amount of her brother-in-law's money, which the robbers took from her. Mr. Dunbar, one of the passengers, as soon as he saw the robbers, got a bottle and played drunk. When one of them came up to him he said, "If you fellers come—hic—hic—come over here—hic—hic—I'll hit yer on the nose—hic—hic—hic—with this bottle—hic." The bandits just supposed he was a penniless drunkard and left him alone, so he saved all his money and had the most money of all the passengers.

A band of Denver citizens formed a posse under George Shoop and went in pursuit of Reynolds and his gang.

The outlaws were camped in the timber about ten miles down on the Platte below South Park. They were always on the alert and expected to be chased, so buried the money and other stolen valuables in a well chosen spot near the road. It is said that even today there are people hunting along the old road for the buried fortune, while others say they know it was found shortly after the execution of Reynolds.

The posse which was familiar with the vicinity around the outlaws' camp, when once on their trail, was not long in finding them.

Reynolds and his men being overpowered and taken at a disadvantage had no other means to save themselves except scatter and take their chances.

Reynolds was shot through the arm, shattering it from the elbow to the wrist, but he and two others escaped. Four of their companions were taken prisoners, while one was killed.

A few days later, Reynolds was suffering so with his arm that he went into Pueblo for medical attention and gave himself up to the authorities there. He was taken to Denver and placed in jail with his four companions. It is said that while he was handcuffed and sitting on a box in front of his cell door, he sang in a clear rich voice and with such a depth of feeling, a beautiful hymn. Being in such contrast to the life he had been living and a song the men seldom heard since leaving their old homes, it touched the hearts of all who heard it.

The outlaws were given a trial under martial law and sentenced to be shot. Owing to the rebellious and antagonistic feeling among the people and the presence of rebels in Denver, who would be expected to interfere, it was decided not to carry out the sentence in Denver.

Therefore, Jim Reynolds and his four remaining comrades were confined in the jail during July and part of August.

August 19th, 1864, when Company A of the 3rd Regiment of Colorado Volunteers was ordered to Fort Lyons, they were also ordered to take the five prisoners along and send them on to headquarters at Fort Leavenworth, Kansas.

The soldiers marched up Cherry creek, conveying the bandits in the ambulance with Henry Crow, assisted by an escort having charge of them. The second day out they were guarded by Sloan and an escort.

Aston Shaw had been kept on guard and escort since the first day out. On the morning of the third day he went to Captain Cree and said, "How does it come, Captain, that I have to be with the prisoners all the time?"

"Shaw, I want a man with them that will keep those fellows prisoners and not let them escape."

"Well, I will tell you this much, Cree, I am not going to herd 'em every night."

"What will you do about it?"

"Go kill the whole bunch."

"That is just what we want done; they were tried and sentenced to be shot. We dared not carry out the sentence in Denver, and sending them to Fort Leavenworth was just a bluff. We are to dispose of them on the road somewhere unknown to anyone. I have sent out Crow and Sloan, but they have failed to carry out orders, so now I will turn them over to you. You understand what you are to do with them."

"I will do it, Captain, if you will let me pick my escort."

"Pick any men you want."

Picking Ad Williamson, Adam Smith, A. Neiland, Oscar Packard, Isaac Beckman and Frank Parks for his escort, Alston Shaw took charge of Jim Reynolds and his companions.

The ambulance containing the condemned prisoners followed the regiment down the Squirrel Creek road. After traveling a few hours Shaw noticed a little bluff that would conceal him from the regiment, so ordered Williamson to drive the ambulance back of the bluff. When the team stopped, he ordered the shackled prisoners out, then turning to Reynolds, he said, "Jim, you are supposed to be the captain of this company. I have your obligations where you were sworn to stay together until your bones bleached on the prairie."

"That was our obligations."

"Jim, this is your finish. If you have anything or any word you want sent to your people, give me their address and I will see that it is done."

"No, I do not want any of my people to know what became of me."

Reynolds, nor any of his companions, would not give a word of information concerning his home or people.

"Jim, you have no show. Here is an order from the commander-in-chief of the western department stating that you have been tried by court martial and sentenced to be shot."

"That is just what I expected and I am ready."

"Would you rather be shot separate or all together?"

"You read our obligations where it said we would stick together until our bones bleached on the prairie, and that is the way I prefer to die."

Shaw placed Reynolds in the center with two of his comrades on each side, then had the escort stand sixteen feet in front of them.

Jim Reynolds knelt on his knees, pushed his hat back from his forehead, folded his arms across his breast and said, "I am ready," being game to the last. But one of his men began to cry and said, "I never killed anybody." Shaw replied, "Remember the story of old dog Tray. You were caught in bad company."

Shaw loaded the guns, putting a blank cartridge in one so the men could not tell whose bullets did the killing. He then ordered them all to fire at the same time on the man to the right. Reloading the guns, he ordered them to fire at the next. They repeated this until all the prisoners were killed.

Just before the orders were carried out, one of the escort dropped his gun and began crying. "Frank, what's wrong?" "Pick up your gun and hold yourself in readiness," commanded Shaw.

To make sure that they were all dead, Ad Williamson shot each in the head with a big brass mounted revolver.

When the execution was over, Neiland, Smith and Shaw took off the shackles and handcuffs, and one of them said, "We will leave you free to carry out the last of your obligations, 'To stick together while your bones bleach on the prairie.'"

The escort just let them lie as they fell and turned on down the road to join the regiment. On the way down they met Captain Cree, who demanded, "Where are those prisoners, Shaw?"

"We stopped down there in a hollow to dig some potatoes and they got away in the brush and we couldn't find them."

Cree whirled his horse and started in pursuit of the escaping prisoners. After a time he returned without them and that night in camp he wrote a report according to Shaw's account of how the prisoners escaped and sent it in to Denver. The disappearance of Jim Reynolds and his gang was published in the Rocky Mountain News, the only newspaper in Colorado at that time, according to Captain Cree's report.

The true statement of the execution was not made known for about twenty years afterward.

The executing of these men was a hard task for Shaw and his escort to do. But it was orders from headquarters and if they failed to carry them out before reaching Fort Lyons, they would have shared the same fate as the outlaws.

A. K. SHAW

CHAPTER VII.

ALSTON KNOX SHAW.

Alston Knox Shaw was born February 11, 1833, at Townson, Norfork county, in Canada West. Though a Canadian by birth, he is really a Holland Yankee. His grandfather on his father's side came over in the Mayflower while his mother's people belonged to the oldest colony in the New England states. From both sides of the family he is a direct descendant of soldiers of Revolutionary fame. His grandmother, Mrs. John Martin, was a cousin of Ethan Allen.

After the states began to get settled the family drifted into Canada, then a new frontier. Being of a frontier-loving class of people, Alston Shaw naturally drifted into the West, where there was a larger scope for a roving and scouting disposition to wander in.

The first fifteen years of Al Shaw's life was spent on his father's ranch in Canada with his nine sisters and six brothers. He then worked as an apprentice for three years in Austin's blacksmith shop in Simcoe.

At the end of the three years, he and another apprentice, John Lemons, formed a partnership and started a shop of their own in the country. They were together about two years, when the restless disposition urged Shaw to move on, so he sold his interest to his partner and got the other boys to take him to Branford, the nearest railway station, a distance of twenty miles. He took the train for Chicago, Ill., then drifted down to Rock Island, up the Mississippi river to Fulton City, finally stopping at Union Grove, Ill., a year. After an absence of two years, he returned to his home in Canada and remained there during the winter and worked his father's and brother's teams in a lumber camp.

The following spring he started westward again and has never gone back to his old home. When he got word that his mother was dangerously ill he started home, but had only gone a day or two's travel across the plains, when word was brought to him that she was dead, so he turned around and went back to the frontier.

He lived at Union Grove two years; then in 1859, he started for Pike's Peak, but only got to Fort Kearney, Neb., when things began to go wrong. He gave away his interest in the outfit and started back to the Missouri river on foot. He worked his way back to Union Grove, Ill. In the spring of '60 he again pulled out for Pike's Peak and in the fall of the same year he arrived in Denver. Shortly afterwards he went to Central City and worked in the mines all winter.

In 1862 he opened a livery barn in Denver. This same year he moved a family and some goods up to Montana, returning to Denver in the spring of '64, when the Indian raids and massacres were starting.

Shaw loaded his wagon and made a start for Montana just about the time martial law was declared. He had only gone a few miles when he was stopped and his teams put into service. He loaned the wagon to a woman and she went to Montana with it. With his teams and wagon gone he was practically "broke," so when the call for volunteers was given in the summer of '64, he enlisted. He served until the regiment was discharged. In the spring of '65 he went to freighting for Colonel Chivington and made thirteen trips across the plains from Fort Leavenworth, Kansas, to Denver.

In 1873 he married and moved to Saguache, Colorado, where he went into the livery business. He had two children, a boy and girl; both died in their childhood. Later he carried the mail to Los Pinos Agency, a distance of forty miles; after this hauled produce into Leadville.

In 1883 he moved over to Ruby, Gunnison county, where he freighted for several years. Coming down on the western slope, he bought a ranch, lived on it four years, then sold out to a sheep man and moved to where Juanita now is and bought another ranch. In 1908 he sold it, and since then he has been knocking around Paonia and Hotchkiss, Colorado, where everyone knows him as Uncle Shaw. He spends his time in caring for and training his five thoroughbred horses.

CHAPTER VIII.

PROCEEDINGS OF COMPANY "A"

As Told by A. K. Shaw.

Company "A" under Captain Theodore Cree and Lieutenants Charles Cass and Al Soper was mustered in at Denver and ordered to go down the Fountain river and take Jim Reynolds and his gang with them. It has been stated in a previous chapter how the regiment disposed of the prisoners.

The Company moved on south, following the old Squirrel Creek road to Colorado City. Here the soldiers were divided into small squads and stationed along the Fountain road from Colorado City to the present site of Pueblo, to protect the settlers and guard the United States mail. During the stop at Fountain, which was all of September and part of October, six soldiers, Albert Neiland, Alston Shaw, Ad Williamson, Ike Bakeman, Joe Connor and Oscar Packard, were detailed to escort for the stage carrying the U. S. mail from Pueblo to Colorado City.

They made three trips a week, going up one day and back the next, making their headquarters at Dick Ooten's ranch near Pueblo.

To break the monotony of camp life the soldiers would stir up a little fun. Company "A" had a team of four unusual jolly fellows, these were Shaw, Neiland, Packard and Jim Taggart. What one could not think of the others would. If all their pranks were related it would make a book itself, so only a few will be told to show how they spent the time when off duty.

In the hills north of Hall's and Turl's ranches on Squirrel Creek, at the foot of the divide, was a herd of cattle on the range. The soldiers discovered the herd and made up their minds to have some fresh meat. Neiland, Shaw and a few of their companions stole and killed a heifer, burying its hide in the sand, and taking the meat into camp.

That evening one of the cattlemen missed one out of his bunch of cattle and after looking around he found tracks in the sand. Following these he came upon a pile of loose sand and suspecting the cause of it, he began to dig and found the hide. Having an idea that the soldiers knew something about it, he immediately hurried into camp and told his troubles to the captain.

Captain Cree was quite sure which soldiers were guilty, but he called them all out and began to question, first the man and then the soldiers, who seemed to know nothing about it. Finally Cree said, "Shaw, what are you going to do about it?"

Shaw studied a moment before replying, "Well, we stole the heifer and she had his brand on all right, and now we are trapped, so there is only one thing for us to do, boys—go down in your pockets and cough up."

After the collection was taken there was fifteen dollars to pay for the fresh meat. The owner thinking it a fairly good price for the heifer went away happy.

The next day Neiland and Shaw were given a layoff from the escort, so wanting a little adventure, they left their horses and stole a couple of the cabby-yard horses (all broken-down and worn-out horses were called cabby-yard horses). After mounting their stolen steeds the two soldiers struck out for Pike's Peak, eight miles from camp for a day's hunt. They did not see any signs of game, so turned back for camp, getting in about noon. Colonel Chivington, who had been inspecting the company and settlements, rode into camp just in time for dinner. He noticed the meat tasted unusually tender and juicy, so asked, "What kind of meat is this?" Shaw answered in an unconcerned sort of way, "Elk," and went on eating.

The Colonel just laughed. Of course, he knew better and also had a strong suspicion where the meat came from, but nothing was said as it was against the discipline of the regiment to play such tricks. It was Colonel Chivington's duty to punish the soldiers if he really knew that they had stolen the meat. But the kind-hearted Colonel sympathized with the volunteers in their struggles, and did not wish to inflict any unnecessary trials on them, and as long as the calf had been paid for, he just played green on the meat question and enjoyed his feast on elk. He was greatly amused at Shaw's way of getting out of what might have been a serious scrape.

One day several of the soldiers took dinner at a farm house about eight miles from their camp. They saw the farmer's wife making butter in the spring house. Oscar Packard took particular notice that there was a "big heap" of butter, and how every bite just called for more. One evening bread was handed to the soldiers without butter, which was very often the case. Oscar suddenly remembered how good the butter tasted a few days before and vowed he would have some for breakfast. When the camp fires had burned low and all was still, Oscar cautiously left camp to pay his respects to the spring house, eight miles away. At first the dogs interfered but he managed to get around them, entering the spring house he found the butter, that was not all, he also found a wolf trap fastened to his heel. The trap had been set and had a double spring on it. Oscar took the butter and started home, the trap following along behind with its own accord, for he could not unfasten it. Arriving in camp about daylight, his comrades relieved him of the butter and trap. They took the trap into Colorado City and traded it for whiskey. This made the soldiers think they had an up-to-date bill of fare for several days.

Things were getting a little too funny, so Captain Cree gave orders not to leave the camp without permission. If they did, they could expect punishment on return.

As usual Neiland and Shaw were first to disobey orders. They left their horses on the picket rope and again stole cabby-yard horses and went on another hunting trip, returning with the same fruitless results but meeting with a different reception in camp.

Captain Cree meant what he said about punishment. Although Al and Bert were favorite soldiers of his he determined to enforce his orders, consequently that night they were put on guard without any supper. These two jolly soldiers took it in good part and were willing to pay for their fun and at the same time to get fun out of their punishment.

The first question before them was how to scheme a way to get something to eat. They were not long in finding a way.

Al went down to the creek and got two strong willows. He and Bert split these on the end and pushed them through the openings on the cabin where the chinking had been knocked out. Then the comrades on the inside put the edge of a tin plate in the end of the willows and when the officers were not looking, the sergeant, who was passing the rations around, would fill up the plates, then Al and Bert would pull them out and enjoy their suppers in their private dining room on the outside.

As the night grew darker, duller grew their tread up and down the picket rope, so just to break the silence and to disturb the slumbers of the other soldiers, these two guards would keep hallooing to each other.

Near the camp was a farm which had been deserted on account of the Indian raids, and the cattle had been driven away by the raiders. About midnight some of the bunch drifted back to their old homes. The clouds had broken away and the night grew lighter, so Al and Bert run the cattle in a corral and got the Company's branding iron, then roped and began branding some of the young stock. Just as they were putting three A's on a two-year-old, one A to represent the Company, one for Albert Neiland and the other for Alston Shaw, they were startled by a stern voice saying, "What are you fellows doing there? Is that the way to guard picket?"

Looking up they saw Captain Cree. Being in need of help and since the Captain was of a venturesome disposition, they talked him into the notion of helping them in their midnight frolic. Cree had been smoked out of his quarters by an antelope head that Shaw had poked down the flue. As long as he was up, he decided to go down to the picket rope and see how the guards were getting along. Coming to the picket and not finding them, he looked around and finally heard a noise in the direction of the corrals. He went down and perched himself on a nearby fence where he could not be seen by the men in the corral and watched the performance before he made his presence known and joined in the fun.

Rations were getting low and they had just the same old things over and over. Oscar Packard, who was noted for his appetite, wanted a change of fare and intended to get it. Down the river about a mile from camp was a nice looking potato patch. Oscar's mouth began to water. "Wouldn't they taste good? Ain't had a good old Irish spud since Adam was a yearling. If I don't get one now my name ain't Packard." So saying, he took a nose bag from his saddle and jumped over the fence into the patch. He was soon busy grubbing out potatoes, so busy was he that he did not notice the farmer approaching, and suddenly he was conscious of an angry and stammering voice trying to order him out of the patch. Oscar was not going to be cheated out of such a square meal so easily, no siree; he had dared too many of the Indians' bullets to let a volley of hot words make him run, so he just went on digging and quietly said, "These spuds are not very big, are they?"

"No—no—n—no, they a—ain't very b——bi—big po—po—po—pota—toes." While the farmer was stammering out the answer, Oscar dug a few more. When he was through digging all the potatoes and was ready to leave, he took a piece of tobacco from his pocket, bit off a chew and offered the angry farmer some. While the farmer was saying, "I d—do—don't ch—ch—chew to—to—bacco. Drop th—th—those po—po—ta—ta—toes." Oscar was over the fence and on his way for camp with his precious sack laden with potatoes.

Although these soldiers were venturesome and mischievous, rough and wild in outward appearance, they were honest to the core and true men through and through.

The following sketches will illustrate that even after many years spent in the wilderness they had not entirely forgotten the lessons learned at home, or the sweet influence of that mother way back there many hundreds of miles in the civilized world.

All up and down the Fountain were homes where the inmates had hurriedly fled, leaving everything just as they were. A soldier who was lacking respect for himself or any one else, entered one of these homes and arrayed himself in one of the girls' finery; he then went down near the camp and promenaded among the soldiers and made light of all girls in general. The other soldiers, remembering sisters or daughters at home, resented the insult thrown at them, so the soldier was taken to the farm house, upon the return of the family, and made to get down on his knees and apologize for his conduct.

Another one, who was not worthy to be called a soldier, would steal little trinkets, that were of no use to him but might be highly valued by the owners as remembrances from home or other keepsakes. Before long those who missed articles became suspicious of him and got permission to search his bundle. As they had expected, the missing articles were found.

Being of a demoralized nature he naturally tried to lie out of it. Five soldiers took him down to the creek and kept dipping him under the water until he confessed. He went into the camp and complained to the Captain of the soldiers' treatment towards him, ending by asking, "Captain, what are you going to do to those five fellows?" The Captain, knowing that the soldiers were justified in their act, replied, "Why, I can't do anything with five men." The soldier said he couldn't either and walked away, deciding he had better leave good enough alone.

A short time after this the Company was ordered back over the divide, down the other side into Bijou Basin. Here the men did not feel so good natured. It was cold and stormy, bedding was scarce and rations were low. Captain Cree had bought straw to feed the horses, but the soldiers used some of it to lie on and cover with their blankets.

There had been more blankets ordered but for some unknown cause they had failed to arrive. The Captain had put a horse blanket on his horse; before a great while he discovered it was gone, so he put another one on it, but it, too, disappeared. Finally he sent an escort around to search the tents. Jim Taggart hurried ahead of the escort and ran into Neiland and Shaw's tent, which was right by a straw stack, and pushed the horse blankets out under the edge of the tent into the straw stack. He did not want his friends to be punished for trying to protect themselves from the cold. The blankets were found, but none of the soldiers knew how they got there.

The Company was stationed here for four weeks and during that time the men and horses suffered a great deal with the cold. It snowed three or four feet after their arrival in the Basin.

The meat supply was getting low again, so Captain Cree and several of the soldiers went out to look for some game. They ran on to some antelope and turned them down the trail into camp. The soldiers all took a shot at them and nearly every tent had an antelope hanging outside.

At last, much to their delight, orders came for the Company to move back down on the Fountain near Dick Ooten's place, forty miles below old Colorado City.

The snow was so deep on the north side of the divide, that it took all of one day for the company to plow its way through the snow and out of the timber. It did not reach the summit before dark, so the cold and tired soldiers were compelled to put their blankets down on the snow and wait until morning. One soldier, who was sick, died during the night. It was supposed that the extreme cold and exposure, together with his weak condition, hurried his death.

Next morning about daylight the company crossed over the divide and reached the Dirty Woman's ranch (so called because the house was always dirty) the second night. The third night found them down on the Fountain, near Ooten's ranch, where they joined some companies that had already arrived, and waited for the others before marching on to Fort Lyons.

JOHN PATTERSON

CHAPTER IX.

JOHN PATTERSON.

John Patterson was born April 1st, 1841, in the northern part of Ireland. At the age of six years he came to Phoenixville, Pennsylvania, with his parents. They remained in Pennsylvania two years, then moved to Iowa. After a short stay here, they crossed the plains and settled at Plattsmouth, Nebraska. John Patterson by this time had grown into young manhood and decided to follow the continual move westward. In the spring of 1860 he landed in Denver, which at that time was the frontier country. He immediately engaged in the freighting business and made twenty round trips across the plains from the Missouri river to Denver. In 1864 he was interested in the first bakery in Denver, and during the same years he was among those who left their personal business and answered the call to fight for the welfare of all the people in general. In the fall of 1865 he went down the Platte river and bought a hay ranch about three miles below where Greeley was located in 1870.

On the sixth of December in 1866, John Patterson was married and seven children were born to them, six girls and one boy. All are married except one.

In 1899 he moved to Hotchkiss, Colorado, where he has since resided. He ran a livery stable for two years, then he entered the mercantile business which he has been engaged in for the past three years.

CHAPTER X.

PROCEEDINGS OF COMPANY "C".

By John Patterson.

Company "C" of the 3rd Regiment of Colorado Volunteers was mustered in at Denver, under Captain Morgan and Lieutenants Weld and Wyman. They were then marched down the Platte river, a mile and a half below Denver, where they camped about two weeks. Their next move was down the Platte about thirty-five or forty miles to Lathrum.

While camped here they had some Indian excitements. Old Friday, a chief of a band of peaceful Indians, whose village was near Fort Collins, was a friend of the white people and always warned them and kept them posted on the moves of the roving bands of warriors.

At this time Old Friday was at State's Station, about a mile from the soldiers' camp. Late one evening he came into camp and told the officers that he thought the Indians were near, for when he was standing on the river bank, the Indians took a shot at him and he jumped in the brush and ran to the soldiers.

The officers ordered out twenty men and horses, also a horse for Old Friday. They went to the State Station and from there Old Friday led them to where he supposed the Indians were.

He guided them down the Platte six or seven miles until they came to Geary's ranch, which was on the north side of the river near the mouth of Crow Creek. When Geary was asked if he had seen any Indians around his place he said, "No, I haven't noticed any but believe there are some around here."

The soldiers scoured the country, but did not find any trace of the raiding foe, so returned to camp about daylight.

The government had about three hundred tons of hay near the present site of Evans, on the opposite side of the river and about three miles from the soldiers' camp. A few nights after Old Friday's excitement, the hay was set afire. The soldiers could see it burning but could not get over to it in time to save it. Next morning they were sent out to look for the Indians that were supposed to have burned the hay. Being unable to find any they went back to Lathrum.

Company "C" was ordered back to Denver and made camp at Fort Weld, a mile out of town, for about a week, awaiting orders to start for Fort Lyons.

When the orders came Company "C" broke camp and started south over the divide near a place called Kit Carson. It was an old camp ground where Kit Carson had his little band of men. The soldiers came down off the divide to Monument Creek, where the town of Monument now stands.

This being late in the fall the snow was so deep that the cavalry had to go ahead and break trail for the wagons and artillery to follow. When they made camp that night it was so cold that a Mexican roustabout froze to death.

From Monument Creek they marched down the Fountain to the present site of Pueblo. The regiment was camped at the foot of a knoll right across the Fountain river from Ooten's. Judge Bradford later had a ranch on the old camping ground of the 3rd Regiment of Colorado Volunteers.

CHAPTER XI.

EST PINOSA, THE MEXICAN DESPERADO.

While the 3rd regiment was waiting at Pueblo for orders to move on to Fort Lyons, a dispatch came to be sent to Fort Garland. Captain Cree was looking for a man to send, when Alston Shaw volunteered to go. After he had his horse saddled and was all prepared to start, Captain Cree came up to him, shook hands and said, "Good bye, Shaw."

Alston asked, "Why, what's wrong?"

"I will tell you, Al, I never expect to see you return."

"What makes you think so?"

"Old Est Pinosa is up on the Sangre de Cristo range and you know what he is doing."

Al Shaw was well aware of Est Pinosa and his crimes, but was willing to take his chances and immediately after breakfast started on his errand.

A short time before this, Est Pinosa was away from home and it was reported that during his absence, some soldiers insulted his wife and daughter. He swore revenge, and to be sure to get the right ones "he would kill every white man crossing the range." But he never robbed anyone, his hatred was so strong against the white people that his only desire was to kill them off.

So numerous were his crimes that Governor Evans offered a reward of fifteen hundred dollars for his head, dead or alive. Tom Tobin was trailing him, intent upon getting the reward.

The first night out from Pueblo, Alston Shaw stopped on Sangre de Cristo range at Sam Laval's place, which was used as a government station. As he rode up to the house, a Texan who was sitting with some Mexicans nearby, said, "Ultro gringo paro" (another foreign dog). Shaw ignored the remark and went on talking with Laval.

The last thing Laval told him when he was starting out again was, "Look out for Est Pinosa, he left here just before you came last night."

After winding around through the foothills all the forenoon, he reached the foot of the main divide about noon and as yet saw no signs of the Mexican. Just as he was beginning to think the way was clear, he was startled by two shots right ahead of him. Dismounting from his horse and cautiously creeping around the bend in the road, he came upon nine Mexicans and naturally thought it was Est Pinosa and some of his friends, and as they had caught sight of him he never expected to get on his horse again, but he made up his mind to die as dear as possible, so he got out both of his revolvers and prepared to fight. The Mexicans seeing that it was just a lone man, showed signs of friendliness and Al Shaw went into their camp and learned that they were with a freight train which was on ahead going to Fort Garland, and they were shooting black birds, hence the cause of their shots. Shaw then told them of Est Pinosa, thus explaining the cause of his precaution. By this time they fully understood each other and had got on friendly terms; they went on to Fort Garland together. As they were almost on top of the range they saw smoke raising up toward the Spanish Peaks. They supposed it was either Indians or the dreaded Mexican and his followers, nevertheless they kept a close look out along the road, taking no chances, as some of the desperadoes might spring out from under ambush and attack them at any time.

In the meantime, while the dispatch carrier was carefully and cautiously making his way over the mountains, ever on the lookout for the revengeful Mexican, Tom Tobin and a friend were just as cautiously trailing after Est Pinosa. As he sneaked down in a pasture, stole a steer and run it back in the hills at the foot of the Spanish Peaks, Tom Tobin was closely following, watching for an opportunity to get the drop on the Mexican and his one companion. Finally when they had butchered the steer and dug a hole in the snow and a little in the ground to build a fire in and cook the meat, Tobin had crept around back of them and just as Est Pinosa turned his back in the direction of Tobin, he fell shot through the back, and Tobin's friend soon killed the other Mexican. The shot did not kill Est Pinosa, so Tobin took his knife and started to cut the Mexican's head off. He began cutting in the back of his neck and the knife was dull so he made slow progress. The dying Mexican said, "Tom, hurry up, that knife is dull."

Alston Shaw rode into Fort Garland, while a poker game was going on in Captain Curley's Dutch Company. One soldier went broke and was going to whip the one who won his money. He got a large pole from a pile of dead timber and was just raising it to strike when the others interfered. He turned onto them with oaths and said, "Why not for you leave me alone; pretty soon me get deadwood on him?" He was in a fighting humor and would undoubtedly have caused some trouble had not a new excitement started in camp. Just as the poker troubles were reaching a crisis, Tom Tobin came riding into Fort Garland with the head of Est Pinosa stuck on the end of a stick and holding it up in sight of all, thus changing affairs in the fort. He got some of his reward then, but it was several years before he got it all.

After safely delivering the dispatch, Shaw started back to the command at Pueblo, and stopped, as before, at Sam Laval's place. Here the Texan again made remarks about the "gringo paro" (the Texan was a rebel and had married a Mexican girl, and not only fell in with their customs, but took up their hatred for the white settlers, whom they always called foreigners).

This time Shaw did not ignore his remarks, but strongly resented them, and said: "You have said enough; now if you have any blood in you, come out and fight." So saying, Shaw got his revolver ready for action in case some of the other Mexicans should resort to treachery. The Texan backed off and began to apologize. The bluff had good effect, during the remainder of Shaw's stay; they were all very careful of what they said.

Much to the surprise of Captain Cree, Alston Shaw rode back into camp at Pueblo on the night of the fourth day out, and was kept busy for awhile giving the particulars of Tobin's trailing of Est Pinosa and the end of the Mexican desperado.

CHAPTER XII.

SAND CREEK FIGHT.

As Told by Patterson and Shaw.

On the morning of the sixteenth day of December, 1864, the Third regiment of Colorado Volunteers moved from Pueblo down the Arkansas to Bent's Fort. Here they made camp the first night. Before leaving the next morning they took Bent's family prisoners, placed a guard over them, and took Bob Bent with them for a guide. He led the soldiers down to Boone's ranch the second day, and the afternoon of the third day they came in sight of Fort Lyons. This was the first that Major Anthony and his soldiers knew there was such a regiment in existence. When he saw the Volunteers coming he sent Captain Sully with an escort out to meet them. Captain Sully demanded who they were and why they were coming to Fort Lyons. Colonel Shoop, commanding officer of the Third regiment of Colorado Volunteers, said: "We are the Third regiment of Colorado Voluteers," and ordered Captain Sully to surrender. He then went into the fort and took Major Anthony and his soldiers prisoners.

The regiment entered the fort, fed their horses, and after the soldiers had their supper, they took the prisoners and marched toward the Indian village.

After following their guide from six in the evening, about daybreak they came in sight of the village. Bob Bent, the guide, pointed down over the ridge and said, "There they are;" then he turned away and began crying, for he knew that his mother, who was a squaw, was in the Indian village, and he was afraid that she would share the same fate as the other Indians. The officers dismissed Bob and let him go back to his home.

About a hundred yards over the ridge, on the north side of the creek from the soldiers, was the Indian village, composed of about one hundred and thirty-three lodges.

The regiment halted under the ridge and sent one company around from the right to circle in back of the Indians, while a company circled around from the left. These two came together north of the village and closed in on their horses, and run them down on the south side of the creek in back of the soldiers. Then the command moved across the creek with the artillery in advance, which moved a little further and on higher ground than the cavalry. They all faced the Indians, who were lined up in front of their lodges, and ordered to dismount.

Colonel Chivington rode down the line of his soldiers, giving them words of encouragement and cheer. He said to them, "Boys, I won't tell you who to kill or who not to, but remember the women and children on the Platte." After Chivington passed on down the line, Colonel Shoop came by with more encouraging words, beginning with, "Boys, you have been anticipating that you would have no opportunity to fight, but your chances look good." Just then a shot came from the ridge above, and the ball shot out over the Indians, who laughed and danced at the soldier's blunder, but the artillery ranged the guns and the second shot took effect. The Indians began to scatter; chiefs, squaws and children ran in every direction, principally for the sand pits they had dug in the sand at the bend of the creek, about a half mile from their lodges. The left wing of the command broke to follow them. As the colonel turned to check them, the soldiers on the right started. The officers lost control over them, for the volunteers, at sight of the Indians, remembered the crimes committed by their hands and were determined to wreak vengeance.

Some of the Indians made for the sand pits, others to the bluffs, while some hid in the tall sand grass and sage brush. There were Indians scattered over hundreds of acres of ground, but the majority were down in the sand pits and there was the principal scene of the fight. Some fought from ambush, some stood in the open and exchanged shot for shot; some struggled in hand-to-hand fights, using knives for weapons; squaws would take their bow and arrows and at every opportunity would down a soldier. No discipline was used; the soldiers had to fight in the savage fashion.

The battle continued all day and by evening the soldiers had completely routed the Indians. What few escaped started for Little Raven's band on Kettle creek.

The volunteers being hungry and tired after marching all night and fighting all day without any food or rest, did not count the dead Indians or look for wounded ones, but searched their lodges for something to eat. All they found was a little dried buffalo meat, and that was all they had for supper. Some of the soldiers went to the creek for water; what little they found trickling through the sand was red with the blood of the Indians. They dug some holes in the sand a short distance below the Indians and the water oozing through the sand became filtered before reaching the holes. The following morning the soldiers had clear water.

In making camp for the night, the officers placed the soldiers in a hollow square; that is, they were so placed as to form a square, with the soldiers facing outwardly in the four directions, so the Indians could not come and surprise them from any direction.

This precaution was taken, for a scout came into camp and said Little Raven's band was near by and an attack was expected before daylight. The transportation wagons had not arrived, so the soldiers had no rations but the buffalo meat, and no beds. They had to rest the best they could out on the open prairie and endure the cold of a mid-winter's night. It is a wonder that any of them were able to sleep, on account of the horrible nerve-racking noise that lasted throughout the night. The whole country seemed to be wreathed in agony; over the ridge came the mournful and lonely howling of the many homeless Indian dogs; further in the distance could be heard the fierce yelping and barking of the coyotes, which had become rabid over the warm odor of the fresh blood. The yelping had the heinous sound of a fiend's chuckle when he is tormenting a victim. The soldiers could almost imagine they saw the glowing and fiery eyes and the foaming and lagging tongues of the beasts as they stealthily crept down on the mournful, homeless little dogs, before nearing the lifeless forms of the Indians, lying in the bed of the creek. Nearer at hand could be heard the whinnying and neighing of the frightened and restless horses, while from the tents the groans of the wounded floated out to the soldiers.

What harsh discord these sounds made—low, pitiful murmurs and heart-rending and woeful howls that filled one with compassion, mingled with the fierce yelping that would turn compassion into fear. All of this on top of the bloody scenes witnessed during the day, and realizing, perhaps, they would face even worse things on the morrow, was enough to make the strongest shudder.

The transportation wagons arrived during the night; so early in the morning the soldiers enjoyed a hearty breakfast. Then they were divided into several squads and sent out to count the dead Indians, and if they should chance onto wounded ones, to put them out of their misery. In searching the Indian lodges, they found two hundred and sixty-three scalps, from little infants up to snowy white ones, from men, women and children of all ages. The bloodthirsty savages were no respecters of people to practice their cruel tortures on. The volunteers found clothing taken from emigrants, tools, guns, trinkets and numerous other things that the Indians had picked up in their raids.

The seven hundred horses captured from the Indians were sent to Fort Lyons in charge of Lieutenant Maire Anna and his company of forty Mexicans.

The soldiers counted between six hundred and seven hundred dead Indians, while the volunteers had about thirty wounded and eleven killed, according to the estimate of some, but this is disputed by others, so the exact number is not known, but the volunteers' loss was very small in comparison to that of the Indians.

Two of the wounded were Colonel Talbot and Pud Wilson; both were shot at the same time and each was shot through the abdomen. They recovered and were back to their work in an incredibly short time.

Late in the afternoon a scout brought word into camp that Little Raven's band had gone down on the Arkansas, so the cavalry and artillery were ordered to follow up his band, while the transportation wagons went by Fort Lyons for more supplies.

CHAPTER XIII.

A FEW INCIDENTS DURING THE FIGHT.

A short distance from the creek was a little gulley, and as Captain Cree was riding past it, he heard sounds of a struggle somewhere in the gully. Turning in the direction of the sounds he saw the Indian chief, Black Kettle, and McFarland, in a hand-to-hand fight with knives.

It was a critical time; each had his knife raised ready to strike; it was a question which would fall, just owing to which knife could be plunged the quickest. Captain Cree took in the situation at a glance, and whirling his horse, darted toward the contestants. Drawing his sword, he ran it into Black Kettle's side, but was just a fraction of a second too late; the Indian's knife had done its deadly work. McFarland and Black Kettle both fell at the same time mortally wounded.

Hughmel Rose had picked up a little papoose that he intended to keep and raise, but when he saw the fight in the gully, he dropped the baby and ran to McFarland's assistance; arriving too late, he turned back to the scene of the main fight. When he went to look for the papoose he found it dead; some of the flying bullets had hit it.

Two soldiers, who had been taken prisoners with Major Anthony's regiment at Fort Lyons, refused to fight the Indians. Once when they were just riding along, they passed an old squaw, one of the soldiers said, "No use to kill her; she is too old to do any more damage." He had no more than said it until he had cause to change his mind. As soon as the soldiers passed her the squaw drew a bow and arrow from under her buffalo robe and sent an arrow into his thigh. He asked his companion to pull it out, then jumping from his horse and picking up a tent pole, he went after the squaw. At first he was going to shoot her, but decided that shooting was too good.

The squaw did not run from him; on the contrary she took her old rusty knife and started out to meet him. She was trembling with rage, her little bead-like eyes were flashing with anger and she came toward him dancing and flourishing her knife, at the same time chattering off some of her lingo.

The soldier waited until she got quite near, when he drew the pole back and struck her full force on the side of the head, killing her instantly.

A young Indian chief came out in the open and exchanged shot for shot with Joe Connors. After a few shots, one of Joe's took effect and the Indian fell. Joe still remained in the open, fully exposed to the arrows, without heeding the warnings of his comrades. Some of the soldiers in the grass back of Connors saw a squaw raise up out of the weeds where the young chief had fallen, and making a target out of Joe. They raised their rifles, but before they could shoot, the squaw's arrow had done its work, and Connors fell, pierced through the lungs. Just as he went down, several reports rang through the air, and the squaw fell in the grass back of where Connors had stood, a victim of one of the rifles.

The killing of the squaws and children may seem inhuman to those not accustomed to the life on the frontier, or not familiar with the dangers and sufferings of the pioneers on account of the savages.

When a squaw comes out and takes her place among the warriors and shoots down the soldiers, should she not take the same consequences? The squaws urged on the massacres and helped to destroy the homes of the settlers. As for the papooses, the soldiers remembered the white children scalped and their brains dashed out and otherwise brutally massacred throughout the country, and also Colonel Harley's quotation, "Remember that mites make lice." If the squaws and papooses were spared it would only be a few years until they would have an uprising and there would be more serious Indian raids and troubles. The squaws of John Smith and Bent were not harmed, as they were wives of white men and naturally joined in with the white people.

Colonels Talbot and Chivington were standing near together when suddenly Talbot fell, and Chivington noticed bullets and arrows falling around him. Upon watching to see where they were coming from, he noticed an Indian head rise up over a soap weed. He shot without success. Finally Jim Beckwith, the noted guide and scout, came along and said, "Let me try that gun, Colonel." Chivington handed him the gun and just as the Indian cautiously and slowly raised his head above the weed, Beckwith fired and struck him right between the eyes.

An Indian medicine man had dug a hole in a sand-bar and placed bags of medicine around it. He would raise up and shoot an arrow at the soldiers; before they could return the shots, he had sunk down in the hole and the bullets would fly over him.

Lieutenant Wyman was sitting on his horse, right in direct range of the medicine man, unconscious of the poisoned arrow being aimed at him. John Patterson saw the lieutenant's danger and called out, "Look out there, Lieutenant." Wyman whirled his horse just in time. The arrow went hissing through the air and lodged in the lieutenant's horse. Wyman was saved, but the horse had to be killed; it was gradually becoming paralyzed from the effect of the poison on the steel point of the arrow that had broken off in the bone of his leg, where it had lodged. The following day, as they were searching among the dead, they found the medicine man huddled up in the hole.

Several shots aimed at him had taken effect, but he plugged the holes up to keep them from bleeding and would go on fighting. The last shot had killed him before he could get the tallow in.

When the fight was raging the hardest, Jim Beckwith started across the flat and suddenly came face to face with Bent. Forgetting the soldiers and Indians around them, or the danger they were in, they only remembered that they were old and dear friends and had never expected to meet again; so in Indian fashion they ran right into each other's arms and wept, being so overcome with joy at the unexpected meeting.

Just as the last sounds of the battle were dying away, one of the soldiers saw a chief stretched out in the grass, face downward. The soldier was anxious to get a scalp of a chief, so sat down on him and began to take his scalp. He was just making good progress when the Indian turned over and a hard struggle ensued, lasting for several minutes, resulting in the soldier going into camp with the much-coveted scalp.

A squad of soldiers had charge of the ambulance and went around gathering up the dead and wounded soldiers. They kept missing Joe Connors and Frank Parks, two wounded soldiers. They were both old friends and comrades of Alston Shaw, so when he saw them fall he had hurried to their assistance and arranged them as comfortably as he could. Long toward evening the soldiers were ordered into camp. Shaw refused to leave Connors and Parks until the ambulance was ready to take his companions. At last he saw an ambulance going up into the gully after McFarland's body, so calling Cobbs over to guard the two wounded soldiers, he went after the ambulance. Cobbs put his horse between them and where any stray Indians might be hiding and he watched the other way. When Shaw returned, Cobbs said, "I believe those Indians took advantage of me while you were gone, and fired those shots." Just as much as to say that if Shaw had been there, the Indians would have been afraid to shoot. Shaw and Cobbs took Joe and Frank into the camp. While passing the bend in the creek, they saw four Indians run up the opposite bank, dance the war dance, and then hurry in the direction of Little Raven's band.

That night, in camp, Joe Connors heard the others talking of a probable attack from Little Raven's band. He called Shaw over and made him promise not to let him fall into the Indians' hands; that if the Indians attacked them, for Shaw to shoot him before the Indians had a chance to get him. Hard as it was to do, Shaw made the promise; but that night, between nine and ten, the Angel of Death relieved him of his promise, and the soul of Joe Connors was taken beyond the reach of fear or dread of any more tortures at the hands of the savages.

Jack Smith, the half-breed leader of the raiding and murderous Indians, was taken prisoner and placed in a tent made of elk hide. The lieutenant in charge made a candle stick of a pocket knife and fastened a candle on the tent pole, so the soldiers on guard could always see the prisoner. Scarcely a man among the volunteers but wanted a chance to take a shot at the leader of the enemy, for they had always remembered the horrible deeds that had been done by his hands or order.

Some of the soldiers had cut a strip of the hide out of the tent to make a pair of leggings; this left an opening in the side of the tent. Alston Shaw crept up to the tent, decoyed the guards away and was watching Smith through the opening in the tent and was just waiting for a good chance to shoot him, when suddenly he was surprised by, "What are you doing here, Shaw?"

"O, just wandering around because I couldn't sleep."

"Now, see here, I know why you are just wandering around; it is for a chance to kill Smith, and I wanted that job myself."

"Well, if you are sure you will do the job up right, I will leave it to you."

Shaw walked away and left the stranger, who was a soldier of another company, to attend to the Indians. Before going very far Shaw heard a shot and knew that the First regiment boy had done his job as he promised. Jack Smith just gave one jump and a war whoop and then fell dead, shot through the heart.

Colonel George Shoop was sitting on some buffalo robes quite a distance from the tent when he heard the shot. Jumping up and hurrying towards the prisoner, he met Shaw on the way and asked him what that shot was. "I guess some of the boys' guns have gone off accidentally." Just then the guard came running up and said, "Some one has killed Jack Smith."

No one ever found out who did the job. Shaw did not recognize the boy who was talking to him by Smith's tent; he just noticed that he belonged to the First company.

When old John Smith, his father, was told of it, he just said, "Well, it serves him right. I sent him East and had him educated. Instead of him coming back and trying to help civilize the Indians, he led them into deeper and lower raids of barbarisms. So he could expect nothing else."

While gathering up the dead, Wise Osborn came upon a wounded Indian, who had his back broke. He raised up the best he could and took a shot at Osborn. Wise said, "I will show you fellows how to kill an Indian." He sat down on the

Indian and took him by the head to hold his head still; then raised the knife to cut his throat, but the Indian knocked his arm and the knife plunged into the ground beside the Indian's head. Wise drew it out and said, "Now lay still, until I cut your throat." It looks brutal in a way, but in another sense of the word it was a merciful act. The Indian was suffering excruciating pain and there was no other help for him; his people were all gone and it was only a question of time until he would die of his injury. Osborn thought, "Why not put him out of his misery?"

CHAPTER XIV.

CAUSE OF THE SAND CREEK FIGHT.

In the year 1861, the Cheyennes and Arapahoes made a treaty with the settlers at Bent's Fort.

Tempting the Indians with vain promises, mystifying them with presents and deluding them into believing they would be benefited, if under the rule of the government, which, undoubtedly, they would, had they submitted to the authority and abided by the laws—in this way the people at Bent's Fort succeeded in getting them to sign away their land east of the mountains.

The Indians had no more than signed away their heritage, than they regretted it, and began negotiations with the other tribes and bands to form a plot to expel the white settlers from the country. This conspiracy just suited the other tribes, as they were all bloodthirsty and wanted a chance to go on the warpath. They began to prepare for an uprising that would last indefinitely, until the white man or the Indian perished.

The bucks and squaws as well, began to gather all the necessities of warfare. They would sneak around and rob the settlers of small articles; sometimes they would hold up the stage coaches, kill the passengers and take their belongings; other times they would massacre families and steal their supplies, firearms and ammunition, until at last they had abundant supplies and large collections of weapons. In other words, they were prepared for a prolonged contest, and waiting for the most opportune time to strike the blow.

In 1862 Governor Evans began to grow suspicious, as he noticed what the Indians were stealing mostly, and anticipated trouble with them. So in his message to the legislature, he put these conditions before them:

"That they were surrounded by a large band of Indians, though seemingly friendly, who might revolt at any time.

"That in case they did, the settlers were in nowise able to defend themselves.

"That they could not expect aid from the general government, as it had sent all of its troops to take part in the rebellion, while the regiments raised in Colorado had been sent into New Mexico to head off the Texans from invading through New Mexico up into Colorado. Therefore, if their anticipations were realized, the only resource was to raise a regiment of volunteers right here at home."

Three months later Acting Governor Elbert received reports of Indian raids along the mail route; horses, provisions and arms were stolen.

In March, 1863, there were extensive depredations throughout the country, especially near the mouth of the Cache la Poudre (cache the powder in, so named by some early French trappers, who, upon leaving the country, buried their powder in the stream). No lives were taken, but vast amounts of provisions, arms, etc., disappeared.

It can be plainly seen that during the last two years, the Indian conspirators were carrying out the obligations of their plot. The people were beginning to realize that trouble was near at hand.

On one occasion a report went into Denver that the Indians were advancing and would burn the town. This threw the people into a panic; they dropped their work and ran in every direction, leaving their homes to find protection in the stronger built buildings. Some were too frightened to run, but hid under boxes in the street. Two soldiers who were not affected by the report, were walking along and talking about their rifles. One of them said, "Let's see how yours works; shoot at that box." But the box suddenly rose up and a voice said, "Don't shoot, I am under here." Looking more closely they saw Billy Keath peeping out from underneath. It was a false alarm, caused by some Mexican cattle herders, who were singing while herding on night watch. Shotridge, a tollgate keeper, who heard them, just supposed that they were Indians and hurried into Denver with the false alarm.

Owing to the extreme danger hovering over them, Governor Evans gave orders for all able-bodied men to leave their work every evening at six o'clock and drill. Henry Teller was put in charge of these men to organize and put them in order for service. Contemplating an attack at Fort Lupton, Captain Browne, with a company he had raised, was sent there to protect that post.

To encourage the men to volunteer their services, Governor Evans issued a proclamation, allowing them to keep what trophies they captured from the Indians, but since there were some peaceful Indians, they had strict orders to molest none except the hostile.

The Cheyennes and Arapahoes were still playing friendly with the officers and soldiers at Fort Lyons. This was only a blind, as they intended to deceive the settlers until they could obtain more supplies and ammunition and give their ponies a chance to fatten and get into better condition. Therefore, they would go into the fort and beg from the officers and trade with the soldiers, and impress upon their minds the friendly feeling that existed between the Indians and the settlers, but on the other hand they were aiding the other bands in preparing for a general massacre of the settlers.

Governor Evans saw the need of more troops and began to appeal to the government for aid. Edwin Stanton, secretary of war, sent back the following answer: "Fight it out among yourselves; we are too busy with more weighty affairs to give you any attention or assistance."

Evans then sent letters, asking for help, to all the superior officers in the military line. Receiving no aid from any direction, he was forced to fall back on his own resources. Chivington was doing all in his power, but his forces were too weak and he was unable to protect the outlying settlements, while Major Downing was just holding his own at Cedar Canon.

Evans at last appealed for troops that could be spared out of New Mexico, but none could be sent to his aid; so, pushed to desperation, he asked the secretary of war for permission to raise a hundred-day regiment of volunteers, which was finally granted him.

In September, 1864, a few Cheyenne Indians were taken before Major Wynkoop, commander of Fort Lyons. They carried a letter asking for peace, providing that peace be made to the Kiowas, Comanches, Arapahoes, Apaches, Sioux and the Cheyennes. After considering the matter and comparing it with the acts of the Indians, the officers concluded that they were negotiating for peace, without the intention of making it. They were just using this plan as a sham to either kill time or throw the white people off their guard, while the Indians proceeded with their preparations.

COL. J. M. CHIVINGTON

CHAPTER XV.

JUSTICE OF THE FIGHT.

This fight and also the stand taken by Colonel Chivington, who was commander-in-chief of the western department, has been condemned by a great many people. In the opinions of some it was but a massacre of the Indians. A crimson blot was put on the record of Chivington by those influenced by tales of irresponsible people who wanted to down him for some political reason, as they were all striving to attain recognition by the political parties raising up to control the state, that they could see looming into prominence in the near future. As the other officers saw his steady rise in the army and in the hearts of the people, the jealous hearted rivals who were aspiring to the same heights, strove to disgrace him in the eyes of the people by branding him with the ignominious fight on Sand Creek.

We will admit that the fight was horrible in every way, not alone on the part of the soldiers but the Indians as well. Though the savages lost the fight, it was not their fault. They would have butchered the soldiers even worse than they were slaughtered had not fate been against them.

As before said, it is our object to show how this battle was unavoidable. Allow us to trace some of the crimes of the savages and see if we would not have done the same. The following are only a few of the many depredations committed by the Indians.

In a previous chapter the massacre of the Hungate family has been described. What could have been more atrocious in every sense of the word?

Just across the line into Kansas, Mrs. Ewbanks, daughter, nephew and a Miss Roper were taken prisoners by the Indians, who ordered Mrs. Ewbanks to leave her baby behind. She refused to do so. The Indians killed the baby and tied the mother's hair to a pony's tail and let her be draggged away. After being rescued from the Indians, Mrs. Ewbanks and daughter died from the effects of injuries inflicted on them by the Indians.

Children were tortured until death relieved them of their agony, men were burned at the stake and suffered other indescribable cruelties that only a bloodthirsty savage could invent; women were carried into captivity, where a worse fate than death awaited them.

Two little boys living near Colorado City were scalped and left alive; whether they died of their injuries or not is not known.

On the Fountain some Indians met two little boys who were driving the cows home and cut their throats, then went up to the house and murdered the rest of the family. James Mock, a boy yet in the 'teens and a neighbor of the unfortunate family, met one of the Indians with a fresh scalp as he was leaving the place. Not knowing how many Indians might be near that he would have to fight, James took his chances, killed the Indian and went on his way unmolested.

Every stage coach was in danger, the driver and passengers never expected to reach the end of the route; they were taking their lives in their own hands when starting upon a journey. Sometimes they got through without any great trouble, but more often the coaches were robbed and at times all the passengers killed.

Words fail to express the suffering and anxiety endured by the settlers. No wonder they were filled with rage and revenge.

Even children who had been disturbed in their slumbers and had to run to the soldiers for protection at any hour of the night, were determined to "get even."

The following story will illustrate the feeling of the children and show how they even feared the Indians and realized the need of protection.

John Shaw, a citizen of Pueblo, had a family of children who had learned to run to the fort when they heard that the Indians were coming and they had also learned to hate the raiding foe that always kept them in such fear. Two of the children, Charley and Ellen, wanted to do their part to revenge themselves on the Indians, so they would climb on a little knoll that had some Mexican graves at the foot of it. The children thinking that they were Indian graves would throw rocks down on them, when their older sister or parents would chide them for it they would say, "We are just getting even with the Injuns."

Charley declared that when he got big he would kill Injuns, and since Ellen could not go, she did the next best and in later years married an officer in the army that was sent in the southwestern part of Colorado to subdue the Indians in that part of the state.

One day when the men were talking about the call for volunteers and how quick they responded, Charley stood and listened to every word and decided he was big enough to fight Indians and hurried home, took down an old gun, nearly as large as himself, oiled and cleaned it and was just leaving the house when his mother saw him and said, "Why, Charley; where are you going?"

"Jest going to fight the bloody Injuns wiv the vunteers." He was very serious about it and was determined to go, and his mother had a hard time to keep him from going.

When little children not yet ten years of age realized the condition of the country and the vast needs of defense, what could be expected of the older ones, who saw even more to raise them up and knew the great importance of subduing the raiding foe?

Even when they had continually asked aid from every known direction they thought it might be available, and was refused it every time, what else could they do but just what they did?

How would the people have judged Evans and Chivington if they stood back and let the country be made more crimson than it was by the blood of the settlers when it was in their power to save them?

It is easy to believe that they would have been judged as cowards, yet those who condemned them for doing as they did would have condemned them just as severely if they had stood back and left the country to the mercy of the savages, and would have been justified in doing so.

It was not the battle alone that caused some of the people to so judge Colonel Chivington. They saw an opportunity to use it as an instrument to aid in furthering their own selfish desires. If Chivington was cashiered, that is, if his office was taken from him, some of these other officers would raise in rank.

Then again, it is said, that some of the officers at Fort Lyons, who had been deceived into believing that the Cheyennes and Arapahoes were friendly, had been making a little money on the side trading with the Indians and of course the Sand Creek fight put an end to this. By cashiering Colonel Chivington, they could shield themselves.

That it was all a put up jop could be plainly seen by just a little of Major Anthony's testimony given at the trial when he said, "Boys, I can help fix up a lie, but when it comes to holding up this fellow (indicating his right hand) and swearing to it, I can't do it."

The results of the trial, which dragged along six months or more, then dropping without accomplishing anything in particular, shows it was only a farce, leaving Governor Evans and Colonel Chivington to wear the stain.

A great many of the old volunteers and pioneers who witnessed the condition of the country and the proceedings of affairs that existed between the officers, Indians, volunteers and settlers say that Evans and Chivington were innocent of the charges against them and carried the burden that rightfully belonged to others.

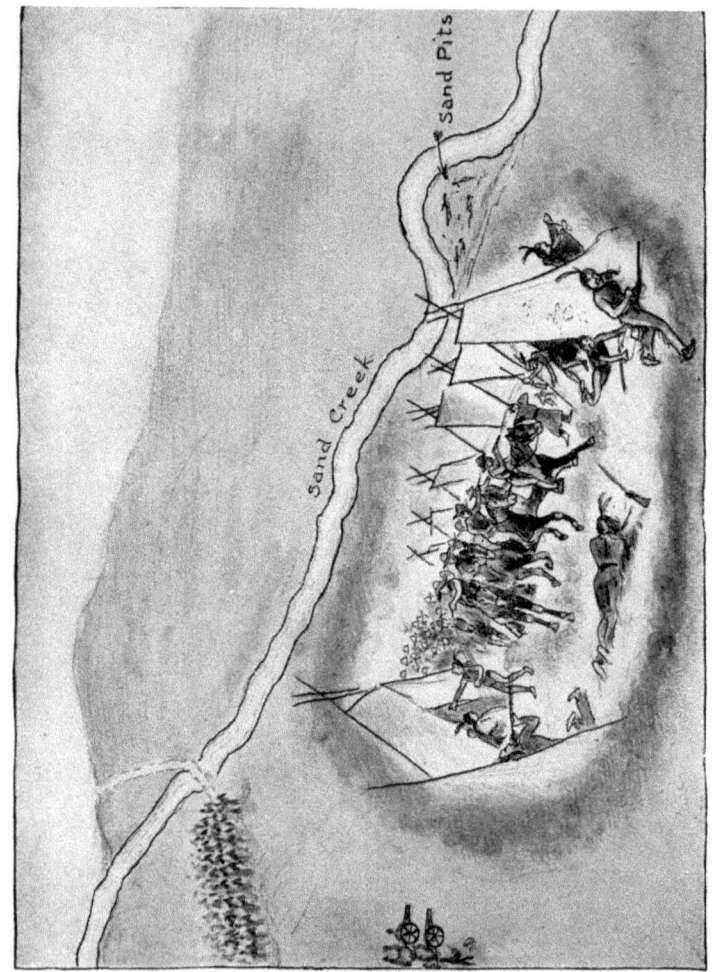

Situation of Indian Tents and the 3rd Colorado Regiment at the Beginning of the Sand Creek Fight

CHAPTER XVI.

SAND CREEK A DECISIVE BATTLE.

Turning over the pages of history we find from beginning to end battles that must decide the progress of civilization, whether it was to raise to the highest standard of mankind or fall into the lowest depths of barbarism.

The following are a few of the deciding battles that have been handed down through the annals of time.

Going back to 490 B. C., we find the battle of Marathon, where the Athenians won the victory over the Persians on the Plains of Marathon. Thus changing the course of early history.

The defeat of the Athenians at Syracuse, 413 B. C., the battle of Arbela, 331 B. C., the battles of the Metaures, 207 B. C., and numerous others decided what the foundation of modern history should be built upon. Had some of these battles resulted in just the opposite the Greek language would have been the root of the French, Spanish and Italian instead of the Latin. The laws of Athens would have been the basis of the laws of the world.

The battle of Hastings in 1066, and Joan of Arc's victory over the English at Orleans in 1429; defeat of Spanish Armada, 1588, were all turning points in history.

Crossing the Atlantic and coming closer home, we have the American victory over Burgoyne at Saratoga, 1777, which meant so much to the colonists. Freedom and liberty of a new and independent nation.

Later when the United States was divided over the slavery and seceding question and the Civil war was to decide the answer, were Lee's army victorious, this glorious land of ours would be divided. But the surrender of Lee at the Appomattox court house was the decisive point in the rebellion and the salvation of the United States.

Studying over these battles and comparing the outcome as it is today and what it might have been had the results been vice versa, we see that "right is might," and, using this argument, we are prepared to class the Sand Creek battle in the list of decisive battles. Consider the facts before the fight and notice the outcome of it and what might have been and see if you cannot agree with us.

The condition of affairs before the battle has already been described, so we need not dwell longer on them, but look at what this western country is today and what it might have been if the Indians had won the Sand Creek fight or if it had never been fought.

The Indians would kill the settlers and push them back towards the east and prevent the growth of the nation, while the white people were fighting among themselves the savages would combine together and gradually crowd eastward on to the unsuspecting people while their troops were away, and perhaps in time they would get control, and instead of this being the land of which we are all so proud, a place of refuge for the oppressed of foreign lands, it would be a heathen and undeveloped land.

The Sand Creek fight was the means of pushing the Indians further west and opening up the frontier and showed whether the wheels of progress should turn and make homes for millions of people and raise the standard of civilization and prosperity higher, or if this west of bountiful wealth, health and untold opportunities should remain a wilderness and barren waste.

There are a great many noted generals and leaders who figured in the decisive battles, such as Miltiades, Xerxes, Alexander, Napoleon, down to Washington, Burgoyne, Grant, Lee, Gates, Sherman and a great many others, all of whom won laurels for themselves and had historians, poets and orators to sing their praises.

This was in a distant and remote country, not many to witness it, but when it is all summed up, in comparison to the population, means and what they had to contend with, did not Governor Evans and Colonel Chivington accomplished just as great a victory? Does not the growth of the West, built by our own fathers appeal as strongly to you as the victory of some foreign lands that are praised by some of our own writers who seem to overlook the struggles, suffering and blood shed in our behalf, by our fathers or grandfathers here at home?

What Colorado is today is really due to Governor Evans for calling out volunteers, and Colonel

Chivington for commanding them as he did, and to the little band of volunteers for being so brave and ready to obey the call of duty. There were also a few fights made later, such as General Forsythe's battle with Roman Nose and his band in eastern Colorado, that helped to pave the way into the West. We must not overlook the services rendered by the scouts in guiding the settlers to new homes and leading the soldiers on to the enemy's camps, although they do not get so much credit as the officers, yet they are indispensable.

These officers, soldiers, scouts and settlers overcame the country's greatest foe, when the United States army refused to do it, and had they waited until the rebellion was over for the government troops to help them, there would not have been many settlers left and it would have thrown the progress of the West back many years.

"So let us, the descendants of those brave volunteers and pioneers, erect a monument of gratitude in our hearts to their memory."

CHAPTER XVII.

THE YELLOW HAIRED BOY.

When the Third regiment arrived at Fort Lyons, all the soldiers were inspected and those not fit for service were left behind.

A boy in Captain Johnston's company was left out because he was too young, not yet eighteen. In appearance he seemed older, being over six feet tall but very thin. He had a fair babyish face framed with curly golden hair that was unusually long and tangled. He seemed to be anxious to take part in the raid against the Indians and when told that he must remain at the fort he was greatly disappointed.

Lieutenant Gilson went to Captain Johnston, "Captain, what am I to do with that boy, he is over there crying and begging to go with us." The Captain studied a few moments before answering, "Well, I guess we might as well let him go; get him the poorest horse out of the cabby yard and that old weather-beaten Mexican saddle there on the fence and an old halter while I find a gun for him."

The Lieutenant did as bidden and the Captain found an old infantry gun that shot a full ounce ball and had a four-inch cartridge. These officers supposed the boy would return to the fort before they had gone very far and they were fixing up to have some sport with him.

As the command marched away, a poor little pony, loaded with the yellow-haired boy and the infantry gun, was wearily dragging along behind the cavalry. When the pony appeared fagged out the boy would walk.

When the command arrived at Sand Creek and the soldiers were ordered to dismount, they had forgotten about the boy, so after the fight commenced in the creek, they were greatly surprised to see a little white and poor Indian pony with a Mexican saddle on and dragging a halter leave the other horses and follow the Indians to the sand pits, where it stood about thirty minutes before any of the shots exchanged hit it. The soldiers wondered where the rider was but naturally supposed that he had been killed at the start.

When the fight was raging the hardest, an object was seen to creep cautiously to the edge on the bank just opposite the soldiers and directly over the Indians. The object would hestitate a moment, then suddenly a loud report similar to a cannon would boom out and a dense smoke would rise up from the south side of the creek. The instant the report was heard, an Indian could be seen to fall. The other Indians would turn and fire into the dense smoke. When the smoke cleared away there was nothing in sight where the object had been.

Every few minutes this was repeated and every time the shots took effect. Finally one of the soldiers was sent around to investigate and see who was there. Nearing the scene of the single-handed artillery, he called out, "You had better leave the place, the soldiers might accidentally overshoot." The yellow haired boy just aimed his old infantry gun down over the bank and went on bombarding the sand pits below and yelled back to the soldier, "O, I guess not," in his usual slow and drawling way.

The old gun was so heavy and the boy so light that at every shot it would kick the boy backwards, thus causing the arrows aimed at him from below to miss their mark.

Upon leaving the battle ground, the yellow-haired boy and two companions were brought suddenly face to face with a huge Indian, who rose up out of the grass a few feet ahead of them and pointed his gun at the yellow-haired boy; there was no time for the boy to aim and fire, so quick as a flash the infantry gun flew threw the air and landed on the Indian, knocking him flat. The boy walked on into camp the most unconcerned one in the regiment.

In dragging the Indians out of the pit on the following morning, twenty-seven were found with an enormous hole torn clear through them that only an infantry gun could make.

When Colonel Chivington was told of the boy's bravery and success, he ordered that the best horse and outfit taken from the Indians be given to him and the Colonel presented the yellow-haired boy with Black Kettle's outfit.

The last the regiment ever saw of the single handed artillery it was going with the Mexicans and horses back to Fort Lyons, but it never got there, nor could any trace be found of it. Shaw, who had taken quite a fancy to the boy, offered a reward for any knowledge of him. The yellow-haired boy disappeared just as mysteriously as he appeared on the scene. Some thought the Mexicans had killed him but the majority believed he went back to his home in Kansas. From what few remarks he made, he left the impression that some of his people had been killed by the Indians and he joined the volunteers to get a better chance for revenge, and accomplishing his purpose, he was ready to return to what relatives and friends he had left back in his old home.

CHAPTER XVIII.

MARCH TO FORT LARNARD.

By A. K. Shaw and John Patterson.

On the afternoon of December the tenth, 1864, the day after the fight, the command was ordered out to follow the Indians of Little Raven's band down on the Arkansas.

The soldiers broke camp and started down Sand Creek until reaching the Arkansas, then they followed down it on forced march.

Flynn Loogstrum's horse gave out, so he waited for Captain Cree to come along, "Say, Captain, my horse has played out, got another one?"

"No, we haven't, and can't get one now; you will have to fall in behind."

"Gosh! Believe I can walk and keep up with this outfit."

He shouldered his gun and started down the road tugging along behind the command, when they stopped Flynn was with them.

When the soldiers saw the camp fires of the Indians several miles down the river, they thought they would be able to rush down on the Indians and take them by surprise, but the night, just before the break of day, was so cold and still that a sound traveled a great distance. The rattling of the artillery as it was taken so fast over the frozen ground, warned the Indians, who mounted their ponies and dashed off toward the bluffs just before the command arrived.

The cavalry started in pursuit, but their horses were hungry and weak, having had but very little feed for several days and they had been on the battle field all the day before and marching all night on forced march. For a time they gave the Indians a lively chase, but before long the horses began to fail, and finally they were all left behind except Shaw and Captain Cree, they kept on racing to see which of them had the best horse and could follow the Indians the farthest. Before long Shaw was riding by himself and Cree acknowledged that Shaw had the best horse and asked to borrow it to ride up to Boone's ranch to see his girl. He did, but Shaw never got the five dollars the Captain promised him.

The command, after resting and feeding their horses, started back to Fort Lyons. They met the transportation wagons on the way coming with fresh supplies. The wagons turned back and went into Fort Lyons with the command, where they waited a few days to rest the horses and repair the wagons before undertaking the march up the Fountain and over the divide down into Denver.

Before leaving Fort Lyons, Alston Shaw was made U. S. deputy marshal to take charge of the seven hundred head of horses and deliver them in to Denver. He left Fort Lyons a day ahead of the command.

CHAPTER XIX.

SHAW AND THE HORSES.

The first night out they made Pueblo. Some time in the night forty horses were stolen. In the morning Shaw sent an escort on with the other horses, while he and Ad. Williamson went to look for the missing ones.

Shaw and Williamson traced the horses up the Little Fountain. After proceeding a few miles, they came upon a Mexican in a thicket of willows. When Shaw questioned him in regard to the missing horses and asked if he had seen any stray ones, the Mexican would answer, "No savy, senor, no savy." The deputy marshal being familiar with the bluffs and deceiving qualities of the Mexicans, thought he not only fully understood the question but also knew the whereabouts of the horses, so he used a stronger method. Turning to Williamson, he said, "Ad., shoot that Mexican; see if he can savy that."

The Mexican undoubtedly did, for he raised his hands and said, "No shootie me, no shootie me."

"Can you tell us where the horses are?"

"Look in the brush," and the Mexican pointed farther up the creek. They followed his advice and found the horses tied in the willows. Shaw sent Williamson on with the horses to overtake the others while he went scouting. He came upon a camp of Ute Indians and stopped there all night. The Indians took a fancy to the scalps he had taken at the Sand Creek fight, so when he was leaving the next morning he gave them the scalps to show his appreciation of the hospitality they had extended to him. The Ute Indians were a peaceful band and feared the others as much as the settlers did. After riding all day he joined the command and the escort with the horses that same night in Colorado City.

Before leaving Pueblo, Major Bowan began drinking. Arriving in Colorado City where more liquor was available, he started in on a good spree. Colonel Chivington noticed the condition he was in and took him upstairs and locked him in his room.

The shrewd Major upon finding himself locked in and his booze all gone, took his sword and unscrewed the door latch.

The soldiers sleeping near the stairway were disturbed by the clink, clink of a sword as it went thumping over the steps. The Major made several trips up to his room carrying the glasses and bottles from the cellar and had a midnight spree all by himself. Next morning he stopped at the head of the stairs, looking down to the soldiers below, said in a very eloquent style that only a practised lawyer or orator could use, "What would Mrs. Bowan say if she saw me now? Would it be, 'There comes that old Bowan drunk again'?" Then more emphatically, "No, never, but instead, 'there comes my dearly beloved husband.'"

The command left that morning to cross the divide, the horses waiting a day longer in Colorado City to give the command a chance to get across before crowding upon them.

The snow was so deep in the mountains that it seemed at first impossible to get over the divide. But with the cavalry horses plunging through the snow and the cannon and wagons ploughing along behind them, they finally succeeded in arriving in Denver about the first of the year, where they received their discharge papers, and the hundred-day volunteers went back to their homes and farms with a stronger assurance that in the future they could till their lands and build up their homes without so great a fear of violence from the Indians.

After the command was safe over the divide, Shaw started across with the horses. They only got up to Mrs. Culberinie's place the first day. The horses were weak and could not travel far at a time. There were four large fine mules in the bunch that Shaw took quite a fancy to, so he hid them out and intended to return for them, but some one else admired those same mules. When Shaw went to get them, he only found a note saying, "I will see you later." But we can be sure he never did.

Mrs. Culberinie had shown such kindness to the escort and gave them such a welcome that upon leaving Shaw presented her daughter, Hersey, with a little pinto pony that the girl had become so attached to.

When the volunteers were called out, Governor Evans had issued a proclamation allowing the soldiers to keep the trophies they captured from the Indians. Shaw remembered this and took advantage of it, so when he arrived in Denver he had eighty-four left out of the seven hundred horses, from these he kept a pair of little pinto ponies and one little white one for himself. Later he gave the pinto team to Major Downing who sent them east.

CHAPTER XX.

LITTLE HAPPENINGS IN DENVER.

No sooner had the command arrived in Denver than A. A. Neiland and Charles Pearson hurried on through Denver not waiting for their discharge papers, and went down to their homes on Henderson's Bar, fifteen miles from Denver. Here they left their horses and returned to Denver for their discharge papers. They were immediately arrested as deserters and put in jail.

When Alston Shaw got into Denver with the horses, one of Neiland's friends went to him and told him of Neiland's and Pearson's trouble and ending by saying, "They will be tried as deserters and suffer the penalty." "O, I guess not," said Shaw and walked away.

Lieutenant Sully was on guard at the jail and was suddenly surprised by a gruff voice, "What have you got those fellows in there for?"

"I don't know as it is any of your business."

"I will make it my business," and Shaw started away in search of some of their comrades.

Soon afterwards Sully was disturbed by a command to let the prisoners out. He hesitated but just for a moment; he saw a battering-ram in the hands of eight men and heard a voice saying, "If you don't let 'em out we will knock the door in." Sully decided the easiest way out of the difficulty was to unlock the door and let Neiland and Pearson out, which he did and nothing was ever heard about the deserters.

The soldiers who had not gotten a horse out of the bunch had been told by Shaw to go get one. But for some reason Bill Youle would not go ask for one nor take one when the other volunteers did.

During the night after getting into Denver, four horses were stolen from the Elephant corral. Shaw placed a guard over the remaining ones and went to look for the others.

He traveled several miles before finding any trace of them. He finally came onto their tracks and after following them a short distance he saw the four horses and two men going up the opposite bank of the gulch. Shaw drew his revolver and ordered them to throw up their hands, which they did. As Shaw drew nearer he recognized one of the men, "Why, Bill," he said, "you foolish fellow; you didn't need to steal those horses, you know you had them coming to you. I followed because I thought some one might have them that had no business with them. Just keep them and go on; I won't interfere." Youle did as bidden and Shaw turned back to Denver.

The army Commander at Fort Leavenworth, Kansas, ignored Evans' proclamation and sent a Mr. Smith out to Denver to take charge of the Indian horses. Upon his arrival in Denver he was sent down to the Elephant corral and told to speak to the Deputy, Shaw, about it. Shaw was just coming out of the gate when a stranger stepped up to him, "Your name is Shaw, I believe."

"Guess you are right."

"You have held out some of those horses for yourself, haven't you?"

"Yes, sir, two of them, down in the barn on Fifteenth street."

"Well, Shaw, I will have to take them as I have orders from headquarters to gather up all the Indian horses and take charge of them."

So saying Smith started in the direction of the barn but Shaw stopped him by saying, "Smith, if you put a hand on either of those horses, I will shoot you so full of holes that you won't hold corn husks."

Instead of going to the barn, Smith went to Auctioneer Clark and asked, "What kind of a fellow is that Shaw?"

"Straight as a string, afraid of nothing, protects his own interest or anyone else who is being run over; stands for whatever he thinks right, stubborn as a mule and always keeps his word."

Smith then told Clark the threat Shaw made and asked his opinion.

"Well," said Clark, "If he said that, my advice is to let him alone, for he always makes good his promise."

Smith wanting to get even for being so baffled on his errand, watched for an opportunity to get revenge.

While he was talking to Clark, Shaw had a soldier to go run the horses down to Neiland's place.

Smith was wandering around in the barn and noticed an old government saddle among Shaw's things. He immediately went and swore out a warrant for Shaw's arrest, charging him of having government property in his possession. The case was taken to U. S. Marshal Joe Davis, who readily saw into the scheme and knew it was just a case of revenge, but coming from an officer from headquarters, Davis had to go through with it even if he believed Shaw was all right. So he put Shaw under eleven thousand dollar bonds and knew while he was doing it that neither Shaw nor his sixteen bondsmen had six bits of their own. What difference did it make, it was only a farce. Smith went back to Fort Leavenworth without any horses, and nothing more was heard of the eleven thousand dollar bond or the sixteen bondsmen.

CHIEF "LITTLE WHITE CLOUD"

CHAPTER XXI.

DEPREDATIONS OF INDIANS ON GEARY'S NEIGHBORS.

Told by J. Patterson.

The Indians made a raid through the country east of the present site of Greeley, stealing horses and cattle and killing the settlers.

Geary had a hundred and fifty horses stolen and a large number were taken from Kempton's ranch at the same time.

Lieutenant J. L. Brush's brother, William Brush, his cousin, J. L. Conway, and a friend, Carlson, were putting up hay on Geary's ranch when they were surprised by the Indians. Next day John Patterson and some of the other neighbors found their bodies lying out in the hot sun. They were so badly decomposed that a door had to be taken down to carry them on. The bodies were placed in a wagon loaded with hay and conveyed to Brush's ranch on Thompson creek for burial.

A group of three families lived within a quarter of a mile of each other. In one of these was a widow, who had the only sod house in the neighborhood. When a report of approaching Indians came to them, these families would all go to Mrs. Wiley's sod house for protection. They went over nearly every night, returning to their homes in the mornings.

Owing to the sneaking and treacherous way the Indians had in coming down on them, the settlers had to use the utmost precaution. They would take turns about in going north of the Platte twice a day scouting for signs of Indians.

Little Geary lived down the river about five miles from this little settlement of three families.

Geary's wife was a squaw, and was always ready to do anything for him or the settlers. Knowing that the Indians would not harm her, he would send her down in the river bottom to set fire to the grass and the smoke would warn the settlers above them to prepare for defense, that the Indians were starting on a raid.

Finally the Indians began to come to Geary's ranch so much that the settlers grew suspicious and thought that perhaps he was in league with the Indians. A few men gathered and went down to

Geary's one night and secretly surrounded his house, to see if they could find out why the Indians came there so much and if he was in league with them.

After waiting outside until the cold got beyond endurance, they left a guard and entered the house; they kept changing the guard so that it would not be too hard on any one person.

Geary was told what they were there for and why they suspected him.

He told the men the Indians were not there very much when he was home but did not know about it during his absence. He also told them that just before they came he heard a pole drop out at the corral and supposing it was Indians sent his wife out to see, but there was none in sight.

About midnight the dogs began to bark but the guard was unable to see anything. The dogs' continual howling showed that something was wrong, and kept the guard on a sharp lookout. At last, piercing through the dark he could see an object, but was not able to distinguish what it was, so called out, "Who comes there?" He repeated it three times and receiving no answer, he fired. The commotion brought the others out of the house and the flash of the shot revealed to them an Indian running away. They all shot at him but the guard's first shot took effect and the Indian fell after running about twenty-five yards. In the timber below the house, Indians could be heard moving in the brush and seen flashing powder to their scout to signal if it was safe for them to come on, receiving no answer they surmised that something was wrong, so left.

Geary let the body of the Indian lay out by the house the rest of the night and the next morning they did not recognize it; he was of a new band in their vicinity. The men all got souvenirs from the Indian. I remember my brother, R. Patterson, got a little white stone in a scabbard. Gerry said that John Kimsey was entitled to the bow and arrows, since he was the guard who shot the Indian. John is living in Evans and I presume he still has the bow and arrows in his possession.

A bridle and several ropes hanging on the trees near the corral showed what the Indians' intentions had been. The settlers saw that Geary was not in league with the Indians, so returned home, fully satisfied with his fidelity.

Grant Ashcroft, a citizen of one of the little settlements, gathered a small band of about ten men and started on a scouting trip. He led them down the river until they came upon a trail, they followed this back into the bluffs and came onto some Indians. The Indians retreated back down towards the river. It being high water season they had to follow the river quite a distance before finding a place to cross. Ashcroft gave them a chase for fifteen miles, about ten miles below Geary's the Indians went over a high bank and the citizens fearing that there might be a village, hesitated. There were only a few Indians with pack horses and the others joined, and all swam across the river together. The white men fired at them but thought they only hit one.

CHAPTER XXII.

CAPTAIN PEACOCK'S FIGHT.

As Told By W. S. Coburn.

In September, 1865, I put up improvements on my ranch and took up my residence there.

About seven o'clock in the morning of the twenty-second day of October, I came down out of the hills where I had been hunting my stock. Just as I came down on the road near my place, I met Captain Peacock, who was crossing the plains with a train of forty-four wagons, hauling the government supplies. He stopped and asked me if I had seen any Indians. I said yes, while out on the hills I ran across three and in the distance I saw a large dust and upon watching it closely I concluded there was about a hundred Indians in the bunch.

Peacock said, "I am the man they are after, they have been following me a hundred miles or more."

I advised him to stay with me until things would quiet down a little, for I had a good defense arranged at my house and could give them good protection. But he persisted in going on. While we were talking, I looked down the road and saw a band of Indians wrecking the telegraph lines. The way they usually did this was to throw a rope around the pole and cut the pole, some then take a number of their ponies and tie their tails together and tie the last one's tail to the rope, then make them start up quick, jerking the pole over, and would cut the wires, thus cutting off all communication to the fort for aid.

My partner and five men got scared out and went up the river to another settlement and left Henry Smith and myself alone. We watched the train go on down the road and waited to see what its fate would be, at the same time getting in readiness to help them should it be necessary.

Peacock doubled the teams and the wagons were driven two abreast, so if attacked, the drivers could jump down between the wagons and thus protect themselves. We were not watching long before we saw the Indians come down out of the bluffs and begin an attack.

After the fight had lasted quite a while the Indians went back in the hills and came down the second time and attacked the train. This time they had left their horses in the hills out of sight and came down on foot to renew the fight. I turned to my companion and said, "Now, Henry, here is our chance."

We cautiously circled over the hills, intending to run their horses away and leave the Indians on foot. The country was very rolling and cut up. Ridges and ravines scattered all over it.

Going down over a ridge, I crept up and looked over into a ravine and saw their horses all tied to a telegraph pole that had been thrown across the mouth of the ravine, and three Indians guarding them.

I was preparing to shoot the Indian who was nearest to me, when suddenly a pony was startled and looked up, this caused the Indian to turn and he saw me on the edge above him, and darted in among the horses before I could fire at him. I said, "The jig is up, Smith." But we fired a few shots to run alarm and the Indians left the attack and ran to their horses. While they were untying their horses, we were hurrying over the ridges down a ravine to the road and turned into the train.

The Indians saw us as we went into the train, but undoubtedly thinking there were more white men in the hills, rode away.

The rough and rolling land gave good opportunities to get away from the Indians, or good places to conceal one's self.

After scouring over the surrounding country and being unable to find any trace of others that might possibly have been with us, the Indians made another attack on the wagons. This last attack began at one in the afternoon and lasted until four. Finally the Indians saw they could not accomplish their aim in capturing the train and rode away.

When we ventured out from the shelter of the wagons, we found one man killed and two wounded out of the sixty-two poorly armed men, while the Indians had eight dead and fifteen wounded.

I later learned that one of the dead Indians was Old Chief Roman Nose. His son, Young Roman Nose, became chief and led the band on just as great raids as his father had.

CHAPTER XXIII.

INDIAN CHARLEY.

By W. S. Coburn.

During the winter of 1865 I had a man and his wife working for me, and one day in December, just about noon, the lady saw some one chasing the pup around the house and exclaimed, "O, look! here is a squaw." The supposed squaw heard her and came up timidly to the door and said, "Me no squaw."

It was a white boy, apparently twelve years of age and could not talk English, only a word once in a while. He looked like he was nearly worn out and was carrying a dead raven. We asked him why he chased the pup, and he answered, "Me hungry; eat him," and he made signs of catching it and eating.

After we had fed him, he told us his story, by means of signs and what little knowledge we had of the Indian language.

As long as he could remember he lived with the Indians. One white squaw in the same band told him that he did not belong to the Indians, and there was a better life for him back in the heap big villages (meaning the eastern cities), and that some day he must run away and find his own people.

One day there was a train of wagons crossing the plains and the Indians sent him and an Indian boy out to spy on it. They followed it until dark and yet it did not make camp. Finally the sayings of the white squaw came into his mind, and the more he thought of his own people, whom he had never seen, the greater grew his desire to see the heap big villages.

When the Indian boy rode back to the lodges, he was alone. The white boy had turned his pony's head toward the north and was hurrying away from the Indian camp. By various ways he obtained food and would sleep out on the prairie some nights; at other times he would find shelter around some of the ranches. He would seldom go near the ranches, for he had been raised to believe the settlers were his worst enemies and that they were cruel and treacherous.

He had wandered about three hundred miles up the Arkansas river when his pony fell in its tracks, ridden to death.

The boy was determined to complete his undertaking, so he bravely started on foot. He did not know how far he had traveled when he reached my place, but had lived three days on the raven.

We named him Indian Charley and kept him three or four months. One day, after he got more used to us and knew he was in friendly hands, he asked me about the fight of Captain Peacock last October.

I told him all about it and took him down where the Indian bodies were lying just as they had fallen. Charley turned them over and called them by name. One he called Roman Nose.

Indian Charley was a bright and intelligent boy, and soon learned to like his new home. He picked up our language quite readily, but had been with the Indians so long that he had some of their traits. Every time he was offended it was, "Me kill; me scalp." On one occasion some one was teasing him about a little girl at one of the neighboring ranches. Charley did not like to be teased, so he grabbed up a gun and said, "Me kill," and was just ready to shoot when one of the men took the gun from him.

The other ranchers up and down the river for about forty miles began to get suspicious and decided that Charley was spying for the Indians. I did not think so, but at last, to ease the minds of my neighbors, I saw I would have to get rid of him.

Colonel King, with the Sixth Missouri cavalry, was starting for St. Louis, and I asked him to take Charley and see what he could do for the boy. King consented to take him. I fixed up a good outfit for him and told him of our arrangements for his welfare. He did not want to leave me, and said, "Tonight, all still, me scalp, take horse and come back." I tried to reason with him, but could not; so I told King about his threat and also his Indian traits, so he would be prepared for any outbreak.

Colonel King arrived in St. Louis with the boy and advertised him. People came from far and near hoping it might be a child they had lost, or one of some of their friends, but they would all leave disappointed, and it began to look as though Indian Charley would not find his own people whom he took such desperate chances to see.

Several years previous to this, a family started across the plains for California. Their people never heard from them directly, but a short time after they started, a brother of the father of the unfortunate family was told that they had all been massacred by the Indians.

When he had heard so much about the unknown boy in St. Louis, he began to think possibly one of his brother's boys might have been spared and taken captive by the Indians. He took some photographs of his brother's family and went to St. Louis. By means of a particular characteristic he was enabled to identify Indian Charley as his brother's youngest child, who was only a baby when they started across the plains.

Charley was taken to his uncle's home in Quincy, Ill., and put in school.

Four years later, when I was standing on a railroad platform, a fine looking young fellow jumped from the train, ran up to me, shook hands and asked me all kinds of questions about myself. I answered his questions and said, "Well, you have got me bested; I don't know you." "Why, don't you remember Indian Charley?" I was greatly surprised and pleased to meet the boy again. We only had a few moments to talk before his train went on. I never saw him again, but have been told since that the Indian traits had been so impressed on his mind that he became a roving and reckless fellow and eventually went to the bad.

CHAPTER XXIV.

LITTLE HORSE AND HIS BAND.

As Told by W. S. Coburn.

An under chief, called Little Horse, brought his band in near Jim Moore's ranch and camped there nearly all winter. They pretended to be on friendly terms with the ranchers, and often went out on hunting trips, but in reality they were communicating with hostile tribes, to let them know the situation and circumstances of the ranchers.

In February they moved camp and took along about fifty head of Moore's horses and mules and started south. Jim Moore went to Fort Sedgwick and got a troop of cavalry of eighty men under Captain Mix and Lieutenant Arms, to follow the Indians. Kelly, Moore, Buffalo John and myself acted as scouts. The Indians had four days start of us when we took their trail. For four hundred miles we followed them, and long since made up our minds that when we did find them we would run into a large band of them. Sure enough, we did.

Spotted Tail, with eight hundred warriors, suddenly appeared before us, and some one in his band shouted to us, "Don't shoot, or I am a goner." Captain Mix put up a flag of truce and Spotted Tail with twenty-six other chiefs, came out to meet the officers and we scouts, to negotiate for terms.

Our horses were facing those of the Indians and stood so close that their heads interlapped, thus placing their riders quite near to each other.

Under Chief Two Strike was next to me, and when the other Indians put out their hands and said, "How"—their way of greeting—Two Strike remained silent and refused to offer me his hand. From then on during the council, I just ignored him. I noticed that during the council Two Strike was nonchalant and grouchy; he would only answer with grunts. I soon learned the cause. Spotted Tail and his old warriors favored peace, while Two Strike and the young warriors were anxious to fight. Since Old Chief Spotted Tail held the highest authority, the others had to submit to his terms. Finally he said if we would leave that part of the country and promise never to return, they would not harm us; if not, we would all be massacred. We accepted the terms and agreed to leave at daylight the following morning and not look any further for Little Horse and his band.

After the council, which lasted three hours, was over, we had a friendly chat with the Indians. Billy Lee, who had shouted to us not to shoot when we first met the Indians, was a trader in Spotted Tail's village and was under the protection of that chief. It was customary with the Indians that if they were attacked by the white people, to kill all the whites who happened to be in the village, whether as a trader or as a captive. Billy Lee acted as interpreter during the council and also the friendly visit we had with them.

Two Strike touched the cartridge in my belt and said, "Heap shoot;" then touched the point of my hunting knife and said, "Ugh! Heap long knife." He wanted to trade me two buffalo robes, valued at $20 each, and a deer hide worth about $10 for my knife. I would not trade with him, and said, "The first thing you would do would be to try that knife on my scalp." He only smiled and grunted, as much as to say, more than likely he would at the first opportunity.

He then noticed the artillery and wanted to see it. I took him around to the cannon and explained how the powder was put in, and how to handle the ram-rod, etc., and finished by saying, "Big noise; heap shoot; kill all Indians around," and at the same time pointed to all the Indians in sight. Two Strike was not interested in the heap big guns any longer and was in a hurry to get back where the other chiefs were.

Just before leaving the Indians, Captain Mix asked Lee if he had any salt in the camp; that they were out of rations except the fresh game they could kill, but had no salt to go with it. Lee said he did not know, and if he had any, he would send a warrior to our camp with it. Two Strike asked how a warrior could get into our camp at night. Captain Mix was off his guard and said, "I will give the guards orders not to fire at any one approaching." Two Strike did not say any more, and we scouts thought his question was extraordinary, since he had taken no interest in the council, and after talking it over, we decided he meant mischief.

When we had arranged camp for the night, we told Captain Mix our opinion of Two Strike's question and actions, and warned him to look out. He did not seem to be very serious concerning it, and said, "There is nothing to fear, boys; we made a treaty with the Indians and they will not break it." We had our doubts about it, and decided to take no risks; accordingly we told the captain our plans and left the camp.

We scouts went to an island in the Republican river, and stayed for the night. We were so situated that we could see the Indian village and also the camp of the soldiers, and if an attack was made we could easily escape. Had we remained in the camp and been attacked, we would all have been massacred, for the Indians were ten to our one.

As the night was darkening and the camp fires were burning low and all the Indians were asleep and not a sound came from the soldiers' camp, Two Strike quietly crawled from his lodge and awoke his five hundred young warriors. They soon laid their plot and were on their horses ready to start for the soldiers, who were unsuspecting any danger. An old warrior was disturbed from his slumbers and upon peeping from his tepee, he saw the act of treachery. He hurried to Spotted Tail and pointed towards the mounted warriors. The old chief grabbed his revolver and started for Two Strike; he placed the revolver against the young chief's breast and ordered him to call back his young warriors, and said, "We made a treaty with those soldiers and don't you dare to break it; if you do I will kill you."

Very much disappointed over failing in his object, Two Strike did as bidden.

At break of day the next morning, we were on our way toward Fort Sedgwick. The trip back was one never to be forgotten. We left the fort with only four days' rations, and were out sixteen days. The last eight days we had only raw buffalo meat without salt.

The weather was stormy and so cold that twenty of the men had their hands and feet frozen. We were in a wild country, no settlers for hundreds of miles around us, so to avoid getting lost we carried the compass in our hands all the time to keep a continual watch of the directions; when one man's hands were cold he would pass the compass on to another one.

After several days of such trying circumstances, the soldiers were beginning to get uneasy; it was the first time most of them ever had such trying experiences. We scouts had been used to many hardships and dangers, so did not mind it so much; but it took all of our nerve and good spirits to cheer up the discouraged soldiers. Captain Mix worried over the hopeless situation, and the burden of the responsibility for the safety of his men so weighed on his mind that he became mentally deranged. The captain was sure they were going the wrong way, and finally the scouts had to threaten to leave him before he would listen to reason. After much persuasion he consented to fully rely on the scouts guiding them back into civilization. Near the last few days the captain came to himself and asked me where we expected to come in on the Platte river. I told him at Bovay's ranch. He bet me all we could eat, cigars and drinks, as soon as we found any settlers, that we would strike the river at Ofellow's point, a distance of sixty miles below Bovay's. I said, "Boys, what shall we do about it?" They said, "Take up the bet, and if you lose we will help you out." So I took the bet.

A few days after this we came onto a little bluff and saw a silver-like thread winding over the prairie in the distance and knew we were nearing the Platte and all began to pick up courage and get in good spirits. We traveled a little farther, then I dismounted and got my field-glasses out of my saddle-bags and looked over the country. I distinguished a farm about four or five miles ahead of us. I called the other scouts and when they looked at it, we decided it was Bovay's. We waited for Captain Mix to come up, and as he studied the surrounding country, he finally agreed with us. It is needless to say that we covered that few miles in a hurry, and the captain stayed good by his bet, and we half-starved creatures sure enjoyed that first night back in civilization. Two or three weeks later Billy Lee came to the fort and told us what a narrow escape the soldiers had that night they camped near Spotted Tail's village.

CHAPTER XXV.

TWO FACE.

By W. S. Coburn.

After his raid down the Platte, where he burned so many farm houses and hay stacks, when he took Mrs. Morris captive and got so good a price for her ransom, Two Face decided that there was good money in stealing and selling white women; so he took it up as a profession.

He went over on the Blue river and captured Mrs. Ewbanks and Miss Roper. After he had them three or four months, and mistreated and abused them as the Indians usually did their captives, Two Face took them to one of the southern forts, supposed to be Fort Lyons, and traded them for provisions and received a good exchange in the trade.

He immediately started to look for another bargain.

This Indian dealt in women like he did in ponies. He would always look for the finest appearing ones and put up the price according to the beauty and style of his captive.

The next victim of Two Face was a Miss Bennett. He was so sure of an unusually good price for her, that he did not lose much time in getting to a fort. The officers gave him a deal that enabled him to retire from business.

By this time Two Face's reputation as a "dealer in women" was spread all over the western country, and every scout, officer and soldier was on the lookout to close a final deal with him.

In the spring of 1866, Two Face took Miss Bennett within a mile of Fort Laramie, Wyoming, and hid her in some willows and placed three Indian guards to watch her, while he went to the fort and made terms for the sale.

Colonel Moonlight, who was in charge of the fort, asked him what he wanted in exchange for his captive. Two Face demanded three thousand pounds of bacon, the same of flour, large quantities of sugar and coffee, and twenty beef steers.

The colonel studied awhile before replying, "I am not sure whether we can spare all that or not, but I will send a sergeant to investigate the commissary and see how much we have. He sent for a sergeant and in the meantime he asked Two Face, "How far is your captive and how long will it take to get her here?"

The Indian said, "One mile, in willows; three guards," and he unconsciously threw out his arm in the direction. The keen colonel noticed the move. By this time the sergeant came in and Moonlight gave him the note to take to the captain. In a few moments he returned with an answer. The colonel, after reading it, turned to Two Face. "I am very sorry, but we cannot trade for your captive; our supplies are too low." The Indian was greatly disappointed over this turn of affairs. He had so planned on a good price for Miss Bennett. He had begun to think that the officers would ransom a white woman, no matter what the cost was, and this was a blow to him, for he thought his business was growing more prosperous on every deal, so this failure caused an enraged and revengeful Indian to leave the fort and return to his captive, who would also feel the disappointment of the deal and more than likely suffer more at the hands of the Indian on account of it.

In the meantime the captain was carrying out the orders in the colonel's note, which were, "Two Face has a woman captive near, about a mile in the southwest; take a few men, go find her and bring the three guards into the fort. If you should meet Two Face on the road, bring him back."

Shortly after Two Face left the fort, the captain returned with Miss Bennett and the "dealer in women."

The colonel asked the captain where the three Indian guards were, and the captain said, "I suppose they got away; anyhow, they are goners," and he said it in such a way that the colonel could easily guess why they were goners.

They attached a chain and ball to Two Face and placed him in the guard house, where he was confined until instructions could be got from Washington. Colonel Moonlight sent the record of Two Face into headquarters at Washington and asked for instructions what to do with him.

All messages were carried over the overland stage coaches, which were owned by Ben Holiday at that time. On account of this slow way of conveyance, it was about three months before the answer got back from Washington.

Colonel Moonlight was noted for his love of liquor, and it so happened that he had a few drinks too many, when the instructions from Washington arrived. The dispatch was:

"Colonel Moonlight, Fort Laramie, Wyoming: You will proceed at once to hang the Indian Chief Two Face, in his chains."

But the colonel's eyes were a little crooked from the effects of too much booze, and he read it, "Hang the Indian chief Two Face with his chains." Upon reading it, the colonel said, "All rite, I do dat rite avay."

He went back to the guard-house and told Two Face he was going to set him free. The old chief was greatly pleased and jumped up with his pipe of peace. The colonel said, "You no understand; I send you to happy hunting grounds." This changed the Indian's countenance.

Colonel Moonlight ordered three wagons to be brought out in an open lot and the tongues raised up and all fastened together, forming a tripod. He then took Two Face out and threw one end of a log chain over the tongues and hooked the other end around his neck; then kicked the box from under the Indian. They let the body of the Indian hang under the tripod formed by the wagon tongues three days.

This ended Two Face's dealing in the woman traffic.

CHAPTER XXVI.

STANDING ELK.

The government was trying to arrange a treaty with the Indians in the northern part, around Fort Laramie, as it did not want to fight with them.

Watson Coburn, a Mark Code and several other ranchmen had a number of horses stolen. Coburn and Code went after them and found a large bunch of horses, and counted seventy-four that had their brand on them.

They went to the officers at the fort and asked them to help recapture the horses. The officers refused to do so, saying that an attempt to get the horses would interfere in making the treaty; but Coburn and Code could put in their claim to the government for the amount at which the horses were valued.

In April, 1866, the government succeeded in making the treaty. A slip of paper, with the Indian's name on it, stating that he belonged to the band that had made the treaty, and no white man should molest him, was given to every Indian who made the treaty.

As soon as the treaty was made, the Indians divided into small bands and scattered all over the country. Some had not gone twenty-five miles from the fort until they made fun of the treaty and started in on their depredations.

A band of eight hundred crossed the river near Watson Coburn's ranch. He did not know for certain if the treaty had been made, so as soon as he saw them approaching, he threw the sand bags in the gate to close up the entrance and got his hired men in readiness for defense, should it be necessary.

The fence around Mr. Coburn's buildings was of sod and stood eight feet high and was two feet thick. He had several port-holes in it; these were two or three feet square in the inner side and sloped to about four inches on the outer. This allowed the men behind the fence to be able to range their rifles over a larger territory and at the same time leaving the outer opening too small for the enemy to shoot through from the distance.

On this occasion, just as he had everything in readiness, he noticed the Indians tying white rags on the end of their arrows and holding them up in plain view of the ranchmen. Coburn at once realized that they were trying to show the flag of truce, so he went out to meet them. They exchanged friendly greeting with him and asked permission to make their camp near his place for a few days. Coburn said they could, and also get water from the stream running through his place.

The Indians soon wanted to begin to swap and trade buffalo robes and furs for coffee, sugar and other supplies that Coburn happened to have.

Every Indian that came to him would reach down in the pocket of his blanket and bring out a small bundle and begin to unwrap it. The process generally took about ten minutes. After they had taken off several feet of rawhide string and some old rags, they would hand out the paper given them by the officers. The Indians prized these passes very highly and were proud of them, which was the cause of such care being given them.

After a few hundred of the Indians had shown Coburn their passes, it was growing tiresome to him, so he began to tell them that he could not read.

He noticed an extra large and distinguished looking Indian, all dressed in gay colors and a magnificent head-piece of feathers, accompanied by a finelooking young squaw, who had two hundred and twelve silver dollars sewed to her blanket. Coburn thought they must be important members of the band and was curious about them, so when they offered to show their passes he was able to read. He discovered that his distinguished caller was Chief Standing Elk, the head chief of all the Cheyenne tribes, and his daughter.

Coburn asked the chief how long the treaty was to last. Standing Elk replied by signs, "One moon, grass so high, so long time (measuring off on his finger); me get heap scalps, heap ponies." He meant that in about time for a new moon the grass would be good and their ponies would get in good condition, then he would be ready for another raid, so break the treaty. Close observation shows that most of the treaties were made by the Indians in the time of the year when their ponies were poor and weak and the Indians were not prepared for fighting. But as soon as spring opens up and the ponies fatten and plenty of wild game could be had, so they need not depend on their stored goods, and when the weather is warm so they can rove around without being burdened with blankets, tepees, etc., they always break their treaties and start on their depredations.

The uncivilized inhabitants of the western plains were shrewd enough when it came to looking after their own interests.

CHAPTER XXVII.

MASSACRE AT FORT PHIL KEARNEY.

Colonel Carrington was in command of four hundred men at Fort Phil Kearney, where they were being tantalized by the Indians.

Chief Red Cloud, ranking chief of the war council, sent about sixty warriors down near the fort to tantalize the soldiers into leaving the fort and start to fighting.

At last Colonel Carrington ordered Captain Fetterman and his company of ninety-two men to go out and run the Indians back into the hills. The Indians kept backing up toward the canon, about a mile from the fort. A scout, who was in the company, thought the Indians had some plot ahead, and tried to warn the captain, but Fetterman was very enthusiastic and anxious that the colonel's orders should be carried out. The scout said he was not going to be caught in any trap and went back to the fort. The soldiers followed the Indians into the canon, and, as if by magic, sixteen hundred warriors sprang up all around them, and in no time they were all scalped and killed. Colonel Carrington and the remaining three hundred men staid in the fort and heard the shots exchanged, but did not go to Fetterman's relief.

A short time after this, Chief Red Cloud came, under a flag of truce, into the fort and told Colonel Carrington about the trap and fight in the canon, and said if the colonel had sent the other soldiers out they would all have been killed. Undoubtedly they would have, since the Indians outnumbered the soldiers.

Red Cloud also told of the bravery of the little twelve-year-old drummer boy in Captain Fetterman's company. While the fight was going on and men were falling all around him, the boy stood on a large rock and drummed away until the last man was killed.

The Indian spoke so highly of the boy and his courage that Carrington asked him why he allowed the boy to be killed if he so admired his bravery and courage. Red Cloud answered that he did not intend to kill the boy, and as soon as he could he was going to save him, but some of the warriors killed him just before the chief reached his side to protect him.

CHAPTER XXVIII.

MEXICAN PETER ARRAGO.

As Told by W. S. Coburn.

A train of wagons was making its way to Montana, in June, 1866, and one night they camped by my place and put two Mexicans on night guard. Late in the night one of the Mexicans mistook the other for an Indian and fired at him. The shot nearly tore his arm off and severely lacerated his chest. The commander of the train asked me to take him and care for him and make him as comfortable as I could and see that he was properly buried, for none of us expected to see him recover.

After offering to pay me for my trouble, the commander went on his way to Montana. On the second day I had the wounded Mexican, I thought he might recover, so sent for the army physician at Lathrum; he would not come, but sent a lot of directions for me.

Five miles below my place was the Home Station, run by Foster. One day, six months previous to Arrago's accident, a misunderstanding arose between four or five of the men, more so between the stage driver and Chub (the only name we knew for him). Chub was shot, and they sent for me. I went down and did all I could for him, but on the second night he died. As I opened the door to go in and see the corpse, a large cat sprang through the door and onto the corpse. He was just beginning to chew it, when I got hold of him and threw him out. It was the only cat in the country for a hundred miles around.

Having had some experience in caring for Chub, I was more able to nurse the wounded Mexican, Peter Arrago.

The fourth day after he was shot another train went by and there were three doctors on it, who had heard of the accident, and stopped to see Arrago. After carefully examining his wounds and holding a consultation, they said that gangrene had set in and he could not live till twelve o'clock that night, and for us to have a grave ready so we could bury him immediately after death.

I got out some tallow dips for candles and took up my post by the Mexican, while Jordan, my partner, went to bed. About eleven o'clock I noticed Peter slowly failing and began to think the doctors' verdict was being fulfilled. Suddenly something happened that made me quite sure of it. As a rule I was not supersitious, but there had been so many strange events on the frontier and I was nearly worn out with my steady watch, night and day, over Peter, and so was easily startled, especially this night, when I expected every breath to be the last.

My house had thick side walls and where the roof came over them, it left an opening. Around the ridge poles at the gable end, I had shelves where I kept my canned goods. A little before midnight, when I thought Peter was dying, I heard a noise on the shelf over the head of the bed, and looking up, I saw the cat from the Home Station sprawled out and looking down as though ready to spring.

I was determined that it should not get at Peter like it did Chub, so I tied it up in a gunnysack and put it out doors. I did not want to kill a neighbor's cat, but I was uneasy, for that was the first it had ever come to my place. Thinking that the cat knew by natural instinct that death was near, I was more sure than ever that Peter was dying. Arousing Jordan, I sent him out to dig the grave, while I did my best to ease the dying Mexican. Again I heard the noise on the shelves and discovered the cat in the same place and position as before. It had got out of the sack, crawled in between the wall and roof, walked across the wall above the bed and crouched down right above Peter's head. This time I nailed him up in a box and put him outside. Jordan finished the grave and went back to bed. I remained by the Mexican, expecting to have to call Jordan at any time to help me. In the early morning Peter came to himself again and asked me to cut his arm off, it was paining him so. I decided that I could not make it any worse and would do as he wished. I sent to the physician at Lathrum and told him, since he would not come and attend the wounded Mexican, why not send the necessary articles and medicine to amputate an arm. The physician made up his mind to come when he thought there might be a chance to save the Mexican. They put Peter in an ambulance and took him to the army hospital at Lathrum.

Six months later Peter came back to my place and said I saved his life. I told him how we had given him up; about the superstition over the cat and the three doctors' advice, ending by saying, "Peter, there is a grave dug out there for you; better go fill it up."

He just answered, "Me no dig; me no fill."

CHAPTER XXIX.

A FEW MINOR EXPERIENCES.

As Told by W. S. Coburn.

In the fall of 1865 I took eight well-armed men who were familiar with Indian fighting, with me after some timber. We went eighty miles up the Lawrence branch of the North Platte, through a very wild country and inhabited with hostile Indians. We were gone sixteen days and had only one scrap with the Indians, and much to our surprise, we all arrived home safe and sound.

This same fall I put up two hundred tons of hay, and all the time we were working at the hay, we were surrounded by the dangers. One day a man, who happened to be in the field alone, was shot off the machine and his team stolen by the Indians. After that a guard was sent out to see that there were no Indians secreted in the field, before I sent the men out to work.

The buffalo and antelope were so numerous over the prairie, that a herd of a thousand head at a time would be grazing right around my fields. They were killed to supply the government stations with meat for the emigrants. There were times when the emigrants were not prepared to hunt, so we scouts generally did the hunting. On account of the Indians always sneaking around in the way, it was necessary for us to take a large supply of cartridges with us. We had no means of carrying them except in our pockets, and they were so heavy they nearly always kept our pockets torn down. I finally grew tired of that and decided to study out a new way. While I was studying, I carelessly wrapped a string around a cartridge and noticed that it held the cartridge firm. It dawned on me that I could fix a belt that way. After I figured it all out, I went to the harness maker at Fort Sedgwick, and said, "Mr. Mitchell, I want you to do a job for me. Take a strip of leather about three or four inches wide and long enough for a belt, then take a buckstring about half inch thick and sew in loops on the belt, just so these cartridges will fit in them snug, and not lose out." I paid him two dollars and fifty cents for making the belt. When I wore it back on the plains, all of my friends greatly admired it and praised it very highly. Some advised me to get a patent on it, but I was over a hundred miles from Denver, and four hundred from Omaha, therefore was unable to go.

Later I went to Fort Sedgwick and asked for Mr. Mitchell. I wanted to tell him of the satisfaction of my belt, in the general opinion of my friends on the plains. But I was told he had invented a cartridge belt, sold the patent for a large sum of money and left the frontier, leaving me the satisfaction of knowing I had told him how to make it, while he got the credit and money for the belt.

In the spring and summer of 1867, the Indians again got so bold and numerous up around Greeley, that freighters refused to load for the west. Four hundred miles of the road to Denver and Greeley was cut off and emigrants and freighters dared not travel. What freight was taken west was raised to twenty cents a pound; grain was twenty and twenty-five cents a pound, while hay was very high, and finally there was none to be had.

Gus Hall, who was injured in the American ranch fight six months before, came back to my ranch with a cork leg and foot. He proposed to me to go in with him and get some cows and capture some buffalo calves and raise them. We got ready the first to the tenth of May, when buffalo calves were due. There was a bunch of twelve or fifteen hundred buffalo cows near my place, where we expected to get what we wanted in a few minutes. On the tenth day of May, we started out with a pair of Mexican mules and a spring wagon to gather the calves. The buffalo shifted around so that we missed them and we kept on going, thinking they had sought the table land above my place. Just before making the rise onto these broad, level table lands, we stopped, and I got out and walked on ahead of the team, so I could see the country and locate the buffalo. To my utmost surprise and consternation, instead of finding the buffalo, there were about a hundred Indians about a mile from us, coming in our direction on the march, as if moving. I did not know if they had seen me or not, and did not care to spend any time to find out, but knew if they found our tracks we would be doomed. One of us took the lines and the other the blacksnake and the way we flew down through those sandhills was a caution. When about half way home we dashed down through a small basin and there we found the buffalo cows and the calves were lying thick all over the ground. We could have loaded up in just a few minutes, but the sight of those Indians had left no desire for anything but to get to a place of safety. After that we were cautious about going out and abandoned the project.

We were out hunting, once after that, and again encountered a band of Indians, but being well mounted, made our escape. I told Gus that he seemed to be unlucky and I should decline to go out with him any more. About two years afterwards Gus Hall and Bill Comstock, with two other men, while out in the cedar canon for wood, were all killed and scalped by the Indians.

The Indians believe that no one can go to the happy hunting ground bald-headed; that is the reason they always scalped the white men, for they did not want them to get in on their happy hunting grounds. They would always try to save their dead before the settlers could scalp them, so they would be sure to enter their heaven.

On June 3rd, 1867, I went out to hunt antelope, and when about half a mile from the house and in plain sight of it, I was surrounded by Indians. They were all on ponies and kept circling around me. The Indians would usually surround a man and induce him to shoot away his ammunition the first thing, then they were sure to get him. I happened to know this, so was saving with mine and intended to make every shot count. It was nearly an hour before I got a good aim and as they ran past me I killed one of their horses. The Indians had seemed to think I did not have any cartridges, and were somewhat surprised at the shot, but as I did not shoot again for nearly an hour, they began to think that I did not have any more, and got reckless. One of them came up behind me and shot an arrow that just buzzed past my ear and stuck in the ground a few feet ahead of me. The Indian then whirled his horse, and just as he started away, I tried my luck, and he raised up and went over his pony's head like a leap-frog. I was getting reckless, too, for I thought I was a goner, and was going to see how many I could send on ahead of me. My attention was drawn towards the Indian

Coburn Surrounded by Indians Within a Half Mile of His Ranch

I had shot, and I noticed that he was not dead, so I got my knife and started for him, but another Indian saw my intention and threw a rope on the wounded Indian and dragged him out of my way. The Indian that was riding the horse I killed, had left the circle and started on a run for the canon, and I was expecting more Indians to arrive at any time. The stage coach drove up to my place and stopped, and the passengers, numbering about twenty, were all watching my fight. But I did not have time to wonder if they would come to my rescue, or to look if the other Indians were coming. The Indian, in dragging the wounded one away, caused the ring to be broken, and I was not long in darting out of it and on my way home as fast as my legs could carry me, expecting at every step to be struck by an arrow. The Indians had me penned in about two hours and a half, all of which time I could feel my hair raising my hat up. About five minutes after I reached the house, I saw the Indian runner return with about forty-seven more. I escaped just in the nick of time. The passengers on the coach were the only people near and they were poorly armed, so would have had no show in helping me against fifty-eight Indians.

That night General Custer, with three hundred soldiers, camped a quarter of a mile from me, and the next morning he asked me if there were any Indians in my neighborhood, and I told him of my experience the day before and thought that they were camped in the cedar canon, as it was the only place near that they could get both wood and water. I also told him that twenty picked men could clean out the bunch, and I would guide them to the canon, which was about twenty-five or thirty miles from my ranch. He then told me that he was not out fighting Indians, but to make treaties with them, and he supposed the band in the canon was a forerunner of a large band of several hundred that had been following him.

One of his soldiers told me about camping one night on the Republican river. A band of Indians camped near and refused to make a treaty. They ordered Custer to move his camp, and fired a few volleys of shot among the soldiers, so Custer had to move. A great many of his soldiers deserted him;

said they would not stand and be targets for the Indians and not have the privilege to defend themselves.

Custer had orders not to shoot at the Indians and he intended to obey orders. He turned back, reported at Fort Sedgwick and went on into Fort Wallace.

CHAPTER XXX.

RED BEAD, ROBERTS AND THE COMANCHES.

Red Bead, a chief, was at Fort Sedgwick, under the protection of the officers in charge. He had won the entire confidence of all at the fort, and at the same time had secret communications with the hostile tribes.

On one occasion Lieutenant Kidder and ten soldiers were sent out to intercept General Custer on his route and deliver some orders. Red Bead said he knew the way and asked to go as their guide. The officers consented. Some time afterwards the bodies of the Lieutenant and his ten men were found near Custer's route. Six months later Red Bead returned to the fort and told quite a tale, how they were surprised by the Indians and the white men killed, while he was taken captive and was treated terribly by his captors, until he managed to escape and get back to the fort. The officers took him in, under their protection and into their confidence, just as they had done before.

One day he asked an officer, that if any of his ponies were stolen, what would they do about it. The officer told him the government would pay him for the ponies if they were stolen, while he was under their protection. About three days later twenty-nine head of the Indian ponies disappeared. John Freal and Watson Coburn happened to be out scouting and saw a bunch of twenty-nine horses and nine Indians coming their way. They hid until the horses got close, then they jumped up and began yelling and shooting, causing a stampede. The Indians, thinking they had run into a bunch of scouts, kept going just as fast as they could, while the two scouts captured three of the horses and had a good laugh at the Indians. They ran the horses down to Coburn's ranch for safe keeping. The officers heard about it and sent a lieutenant and an escort after them. Coburn bluffed them out and they went back without the ponies. But Red Bead was paid for the ponies, that his own band stole for him.

The Comanches were considered about the hardest fighters among the Indians, but as a usual thing they confined nearly all of their depredations to stealing stock, only occasionally killing and scalping the settlers.

The ranchers were far apart and had to be almost self-supporting. When one was raided the others were notified and they would gather and follow the raiders. The following incident was told by C. F. Roberts, who was an early settler in Texas, and had many trying experiences with the Comanches.

This particular time seven Indians had stolen a number of head of stock and started toward the west. The owner sent out messages to the other settlers to meet at a certain elevation and they would combine and go after them. They began to meet, fifteen and twenty at a time, and when they had a large enough number they started in pursuit of the Indians.

They overtook the Indians and recaptured the stock and cornered the Indians in a hole in a wash-out. The men didn't dare go to the edge of the hole and look in, for the Indians could get a good shot at them. The men would go back and hold council and decide to storm the hole, but they all knew if they did some would be sure to get killed, so they would back out. They counciled, and started a charge several times, and every time would back out. For some time they had not heard any noise in the hole and had almost concluded that the Indians had found some way out, without the men seeing them, but none of them would risk taking a peep to be sure about it. About three o'clock in the afternoon, when they were getting uneasy and wondering what to do, they saw a large dark cloud coming over the western horizon. In a few minutes it began to rain; then suddenly the water rushed in a torrent down the washout. There had been a cloudburst above them. When they were able to reach the hole, they dragged out seven drowned Indians. One of them was a squaw, who had taken a warrior's place.

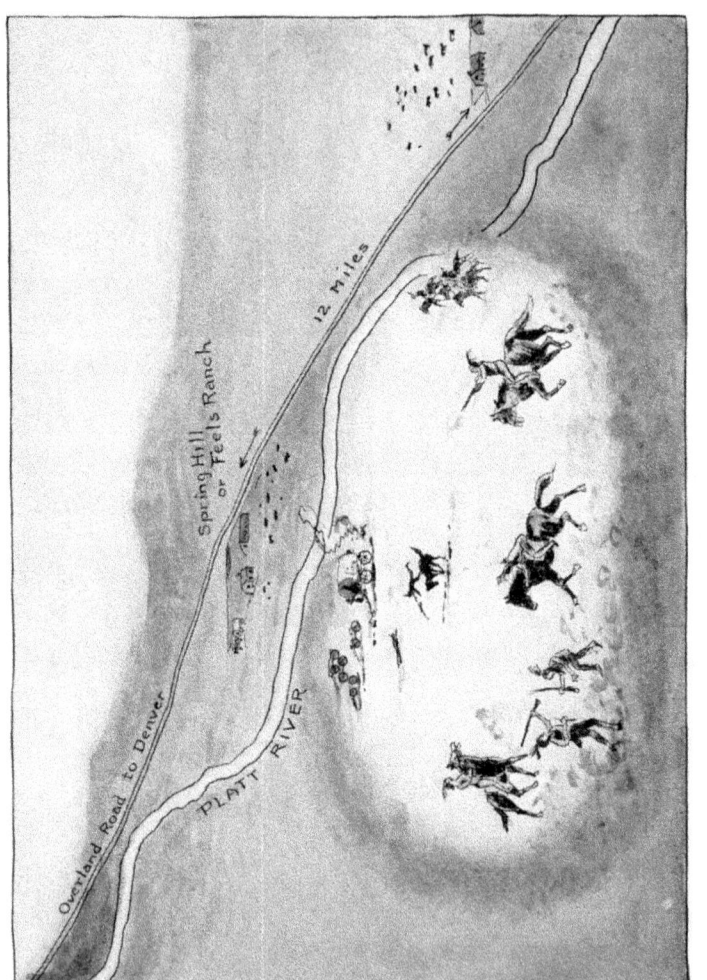

FIGHT WITH EAGLE CLAW

CHAPTER XXXI.

FIGHT WITH EAGLE CLAW.

By W. S. Coburn.

On the north side of the Platte river there was a distance of three hundred miles where there were no roads or settlements. There was plenty of good grass on the north side, owing to there being no travel, and for that reason Arthur Lewis went down the north side and camped, June 3, 1867, across from the Spring Hill ranch, twelve miles below Mr. Coburn's ranch. Mr. Coburn tells the following story about their fight with Chief Eagle Claw:

One of our cows had run away, and I went down to the Spring Hill ranch after it. I stayed for dinner, then immediately afterwards started home. I had gone about three miles when I rode over a ridge, and looking across the river, I saw nine horsemen riding towards Lewis' wagon and oxen. I rode back to the ranch and asked Mr Freal: "Are there any soldiers out from the fort?" He said he did not know of any. I got my glasses and looked at the horsemen and discovered that they were Indians, coming down from the bluffs toward the wagons, and we realized at once there was going to be an attack. Arthur Lewis had left the wagon and was somewhere around the ranch. I found him and showed the Indians to him and asked if there was any one with the wagons. He said, "Yes, I left a young fellow, George Teal, over there."

"Did you leave any guns or ammunition in the wagon?" I asked him.

"Yes, seven guns and plenty of ammunition."

There were eight men and myself at the ranch, and I suggested that we take the boat and cross over to Teal's assistance. The others all hesitated, and then began to make excuses. They couldn't all leave the ranch, and some couldn't swim, in case the boat should tip over, were some of their excuses.

By this time I was getting vexed with them and said, "I believe you fellows are all cowards and afraid to go. I know it is a risky business and all that, but we can't stand here and watch the Indians get that man without us taking a chance to help him. I am going; is anyone coming with me?"

Tom Fought, who used to work for me and was in several hard fights with me, and Henry Freal spoke up, "Take the lead, Coburn; we will follow you."

The river was high and running swift, so we towed the boat up stream quit a distance, that we might be able to land on the opposite bank with the wagon between us and the Indians. Tom rowed the boat, Henry steered it, and I sat with my rifle ready in case it would be necessary to use it.

In the meantime, Teal had seen the Indians approaching and got in the covered wagon, tied the canvass sheets together at both ends, loaded up his seven guns and waited for them. When they began to fire at the wagons, Teal just peppered it back into them. The Indians, seeing that they had a harder proposition than they expected, sent a runner back to their camp for more warriors.

The current was so swift, it was taking us below the wagon, and before long the Indians caught sight of us and left the wagon and ran down the bank, waiting for us to get in rifle range, then fire into us. When we were nearing the bank, I saw an Indian with a rifle, that looked about nine feet long to me just then, and he was leveling it in our direction, so I told the boys to drop flat in the boat, and just as I started to drop, crack! went that rifle, and the bullet grazed across my temple. I dropped into the river. I was stunned several minutes and when I gradually came to myself, I was standing in water waist deep and holding onto my rifle, which was also standing in the water. I looked around and saw the boat drifting down stream, and as I was collecting my thoughts as to how I got there, the accident came to my mind and I said to myself, "Well, you have been shot, but where?" and while looking for the bullet hole, I happened to look up and saw an Indian hiding behind a rock, loading a gun. I thought, "Old fellow, I'll just beat you to it." I took my gun out of the river, poured the water out of it and had it ready, so just as I saw the Indian edge around the rock and that nine-foot gun aimed at me, I fired. The Indian turned a somersault and limped away. The boys in the boat looked around and I motioned them to pull ashore. One of them landed and the other came back after me. We then got under the bank and taking the boat with us, started toward the wagon. As the Indians saw they could not get to us while we were under the bank, they hurried back to the wagon, intending to get Teal and raid the wagon before we got there. By this time fourteen more Indians had come down from their camp, and a runner had been sent for still more, so their number was increased to fifty-eight, while there were only four of us.

Teal could not imagine what the commotion was outside, as he could not see out, and never once thought that it was some one coming to his aid, since he knew there was no white man for a hundred miles on that side of the river, and he did not think any one would dare to cross the river when it was so high, and a mob of Indians waiting for them to land. When he heard the Indians returning to the wagon he peeped out and saw us back of him near the bank. He jumped from his hiding place and joined us. We had got there just in time, for he had only three cartridges left, and in another five minutes the Indians would have had him.

We kept up a pitched fight for quite a while, when it died down a little and we had time to look around, we noticed one Indian with the long rifle, making his way to the bank. He was out of rifle reach, so all we could do was to keep watch on him. I surmised that his intention was to get under the bank, crawl up and let our boat down stream and leave us without any means of getting back to the ranch, then while the others held our attention in front, he would pick us off one at a time. While we were watching the Indian and talking about his intentions the other Indians had fallen back to council. Suddenly they charged down on us, yelling and shooting. For ten or fifteen minutes they took our entire attention and when we had a chance to look for the Indian whom we had seen making his way to the river, he had disappeared. About two hundred yards below us was a sharp bend in the bank. I thought he might be hiding back of that until the others could make another charge, then he could get up back of us. I said, "Boys, watch in the grass below here for him and keep an eye on the others; I am going to get under the bank, take my chances and meet that Indian at the turn and see if I can't head him off."

I managed to drop over the bank unseen, and crawled to the turn. I then stopped to load my gun, and crouched down, ready to spring, but he did not come, and as I did not want to waste any time, I leaped around the turn, thinking that I would take him at a disadvantage and get the drop on him. But he wasn't there. I cautiously peeped up over the bank and saw a black head raised up out of a buffalo wallow (a place where the buffalo have pawed out a hole to catch rain.water in) a short distance away. Before I could shoot, it dropped out of sight. Again it raised up and took a glance toward the wagon, as though measuring the distance, then dropped down in the grass. I leveled my rifle over the bank and waited. Suddenly he sprang out of the wallow with his gun to his shoulder, aimed at one of the boys back of the wagon, who was unaware of his danger and busy watching the Indians in front. By the time the Indian was on his feet, I fired and he fell. To be sure that he was dead, I leaped up the bank with knife in my hand, and started for him. At the same time Tom came running from the wagon and said, "That is my Indian." We looked for the bullets and mine struck him square and went clear through, while Tom's hit him on the left wrist just where it was bent in holding the barrel of the rifle, and as the Indian was turned sideways toward Tom, the bullet went on into the left side of his chest and lodged against the skin on the right shoulder. The boys had followed my advice, and Tom watched in the grass, while George and Henry stood off those in front.

The Indian we killed was Eagle Claw, and when the others saw that their chief was dead, refused to fight any more and went to their camp. The Indian camp was about a half mile from the wagon and I watched them through my glasses, and saw they had three dead and eight wounded. Fearing they might come down in the night and attack again, we decided to make them leave entirely.

George Teal and Henry Freal remained at the wagon, so if the Indians should surround us they could break the ring. Tom Fought and I went toward the camp and on the way we picked up two buffalo heads and took them with us. When we got within rifle range, we laid down in a wallow and placed the heads in front of us and opened fire into the camp. The Indians would not return the shots, but threw their dead and wounded across the ponies and left camp just as it was. We got all the buffalo robes, blankets and trinkets that the boat would hold. We took a large eagle claw, that was on a string of beads, from around the chief's neck, two five-cent pieces that were fastened in his ears with brass rings and a large brass ring out of his nose. He had a bag on a string around his neck that they called a medicine bag, and believed that it would protect him from all harm. We opened the bag just to see what was in it, and found it full of a baby's hair. We loaded the boat and crossed back to the Spring Hill ranch just at sunset.

The stage route passed the ranch and on this day the stage was going by as we were fighting, and stopped for four hours watching us. The passengers not being used to such sights, were awfully excited. Among them was a son of Jefferson C. Davis, and he wrote back to his father a description of the fight and termed the frontiersmen as barbarians and called the Indians those poor abused people. There was good excuse for him, for at that time he was what we called a tenderfoot, and if he stayed out west very long he would soon learn. But his lesson came sooner than we had expected. The morning following our fight, as the stage was going on to Moore's place, it was attacked by the Indians and one of the leaders of the six-horse team was killed and Davis' son was shot in the groin, and for two months we did not expect to see him get well. The Indians changed his mind for him concerning themselves, and he wrote another letter to his father about the cruel savages and the brave frontiersmen. A letter entirely different from the first.

CHAPTER XXXII.

FIGHT OF GENERAL FORSYTH.

As Told by A. K. Shaw.

In the year of 1868, General Forsyth, assisted by Lieutenant Beecher and Scouts Grover and McCall, had charge of fifty-one men in the eastern part of Colorado. They were certain of an attack and had no more than completed their preparations for a defense than young Chief Roman Nose, a perfect specimen of a savage leader, being six feet and three inches tall and sinewy and slim, and carrying himself with a daring and reckless movement, led his band of a thousand warriors just a little beyond rifle range of the soldiers. Two squads of these were placed at each end of the island and kept up a continual crossfire, so that the soldiers did not dare to raise in their rifle pits to fire at the oncoming forces that were charging down on them from in front, so the bullets were falling thick all around the soldiers. Fortunately for the soldiers, that once the chargers came within range of the bullets of their men on the island, they would have to cease firing. The general noticed this, so was waiting for the break in the firing. His soldiers had turned in their rifle pits, their rifles to their shoulders ready to spring up and fire as soon as the order was given. They were all impatiently waiting.

Before a great while the cross-fire ceased and the soldiers had their chance. General Forsyth said, "Now," and Beecher, McCall and Grover repeated the order. The soldiers rose as one man and sent seven consecutive volleys into the charging horde of savages. The first and second volleys were answered with yells from the savages, as they continued towards the rifle pits, but the third was followed by fewer shouts and gaps began to show in their ranks. But still they kept bravely pushing on to the soldiers, Roman Nose leading them and wildly waving his rifle at them to come on, and shouting his defiant war cry. At the fourth volley, their medicine man, who was leading one of their columns, went down. This checked the others for an instant; then they rushed on with renewed energy and force. The fifth volley thinned their ranks, and with the sixth, Chief

Roman Nose and his horse fell together, both mortally wounded.

A few feet more and the savages would be upon the soldiers, but the column hesitates and shows signs of weakness; the soldiers take advantage of them and poured the seventh volley into their ranks, just as some of the warriors had reached the edge of the island. Then, with ringing cheers, the frontiersmen springing quickly to their feet, poured the contents of their revolvers into the very faces of the onrushing mounted warriors. The Indians, completely cowered and defeated, divided, and laying low over their ponies, hurried to get out of reach of the soldiers' revolvers and to a place of safety.

There were about eight soldiers killed and twelve wounded. General Forsyth was wounded three times, but dragged himself around to care for the wounded soldiers. Lieutenant Beecher was shot in the side, and simply said, "General, I have got my death wound," then murmured something about "poor mother," and died as bravely and unflinchingly as he had fought.

The dead horses were unsaddled and the saddles used to strengthen the fortifications, and pieces of the horses were buried to keep for the soldiers to subsist on. The meat had to be eaten raw, but fortunately there was plenty of good water. The soldiers, being nearly exhausted, slept throughout the night, but the next day was so hot that the wounded ones suffered intensely. It was a gloomy day, without food, but raw horse meat; no comfort for the wounded and no hope of ever getting away; and in the Indian camp near by the squaws were beating drums and keeping up a steady death chant.

The soldiers dared not venture from behind their fortifications, for they would have no chance whatever; the Indians were waiting for them, and such a few, burdened with their wounded comrades, could not protect themselves. They must wait and let fate take its course.

General Forsyth had sent out two messengers to carry dispatches to the officers at Fort Wallace, telling of their hopeless condition and asking for help. But the messengers were unable to get past the Indian pickets, so returned. The day after the fight he sent two more, with full particulars of the fight, the wounded, and their trying circumstances. In the meantime the soldiers were growing weaker and more hopeless. On the fourth day the meat had become putrid, but one of the soldiers killed a wolf, which helped them to hold out a little longer.

Forsyth's wound was getting very painful and he asked the soldiers to cut the bullet out, but it being near the femoral artery they were afraid to undertake it, so the general took his razor and cut it out himself. Later his leg was jarred and the broken bone protruded through the flesh. On the sixth day Forsyth called the well soldiers to him and told them to try and save themselves; the wounded ones would stay and take their chances, they were about done for anyway. There was silence for a few moments, then the men said, "Never! Never! We will stand by you till the end, general." And McCall said, "We have fought together, and, by heavens, if need be, we can die together."

Thus showing the faithfulness and self-sacrifice of the scouts and soldiers on the frontier.

The next two days seemed to be almost interminable, as there was so much suffering and misery among the slowly starving and dying soldiers. On the morning of the ninth day, one of the soldiers jumped up and said, "There are some objects on the hills in the distance." All that were able leaped to their feet and strained their eyes to see what it was. Finally a scout said, "By the heavens above us, it is an ambulance." The strain was over. The two messengers had succeeded in meeting Colonel Carpenter with the Tenth cavalry and he hastened to their rescue.

Though the fight was a thousand to fifty-one, the white men won in the end, in spite of the uneven numbers, the hardships and suffering and the disadvantages of the soldiers.

CHIEF "YELLOWHAIR"

CHAPTER XXXIII.

A TRIP INTO MONTANA.

As Told by A. K. Shaw.

In November, 1863, I left Denver with a two-horse team and some of my truck, and headed for Helena, Montana. A short time afterwards I took four or five wagons and men and went near Banick City, put up a log house and started a station. It was while here that I got acquainted with some of the road agents and familiar with their plans and tricks.

The Indians were not our only enemies; we lost a lot through the road agents, who were principally the criminals and jail breakers that escaped from the East and took refuge in our western wilderness, where there was no law, and, as they supposed, they could have things their own way. But they got fooled. We formed vigilant parties to protect ourselves, and no more thought of stringing up an outlaw who molested us than we did of scalping a redskin who had killed our neighbor and destroyed our property.

Just to show you how we did it, I will tell you of some of the road agents I ran across while on my trip to Montana.

In that part of Montana, gold was found in great quantities, and a large gang of men were getting out the gold dust and going back to the states, so there was a continual come and go.

The outlaws soon saw a chance for easy money and after the miners got the gold and started on the road home, they were often waylaid and robbed, generally killed.

Henry Plummer had been appointed sheriff, but the people noticed that the road agents were just as bad as ever, and soon discovered that Plummer was their leader and playing into their hands.

On one occasion Jack Oliver, Jack Hughes and Sloan took several mule teams and loads of groceries and liquor to a station about sixty miles from my station. They got a large amount of gold dust in exchange for their loads. Being afraid to try to carry it home, they traded it for greenbacks and put them in several envelopes and addressed them to different people in Denver, and scattered them out among their drivers, just as though it was letters they were carrying back.

The road agents always had spies out, and one of them got onto how the money was being carried. As the teams were quite a distance out on the road they were held up and the money taken from the drivers. When the robbers got to the last wagon, Jack Hughes and Sloan raised up from under the canvas cover and opened fire on them. The robbers dropped the envelopes and ran. The two who attacked the last wagon were severely wounded, but managed to escape.

Sloan, Hughes and their men went on into the next town and reported. Five vigilantes, headed by John Featherson, started in pursuit.

A few nights before a man by the name of Pease stopped at my place and had turned his horse loose to go to water. The horse failed to come back to the feed and we scoured all around the place, but found no trace of it. When the outlaws held up Sloan's party they had a horse that Sloan recognized as Pease's. He recaptured it and returned it to its owner.

As the vigilantes were scouring the country for the road agents, they noticed smoke curling up out of the willows in the distance and turned that way.

John Wagner and Ned Ray, the two outlaws wounded by Sloan and Hughes, got as far as the willows and gave out, on account of the pain and loss of blood resulting from their wounds. They stopped and built a fire and waited, taking their chances for either some of their companions or the vigilantes finding them first.

When found by the latter, they were nearly starved, their wounds swollen and hands and feet badly frozen. They were brought to my cabin and cared for until something was decided upon. There was no bed for Wagner, so I took him in with me. The boys tried to talk me out of it, but he was human and suffering, and I knew he could not harm me, he being in such a condition.

The vigilantes strung Wagner up three times to make him confess and tell who his comrades were. The ones he named were Jack Gallager, Henry Plummer, Club-Foot George, Ned Ray, Spanish Pete and several others, whose names I have forgotten.

Spanish Pete was a desperate and daring fellow. He always said he would never be taken alive, but would always save one shot for himself when cornered. While trying to capture Spanish Pete, Cubbly was shot in the hip and Featherson was grazed across the side of the head; his hair was shaved off by a bullet from the temple back. Pete hid in a log house that was built with logs about six to eight inches in diameter. He was well armed and protected, and at first no one could get near enough to make an opening in the building. At last one of the men thought of a little army howitzer that had been given to a family to take across the plains. He got it and shot a four-pound ball through the walls of the cabin. The ball went through both walls of that cabin and on into my cabin and lodged in a sack of flour.

Durant, who had had some serious trouble in the past with Pete, knocked down the door and shot him twice with a double-barreled shotgun. I believe that Pete was dead before Durant shot him, for he was crouched down in a corner and I noticed a hole in his temple with powder burns around it, and I think he carried out his threat.

The vigilantes took his body and hung it on Mrs. Moser's clothes line scalene; then they just riddled it with bullets. Later the body was burned on some poles taken from the log house.

Three more were hanged that night. Henry Plummer was one of them. He was the first to hang on the gallows that he had built to hang his prisoners on during his term of sheriff, but his term expired before he had the opportunity to hang any one.

Slade, Club-Foot George, Jack Gallager and Boone Helm were taken to Helena and hanged the next morning. As they were all standing on the boxes with the noose around their necks, Helm noticed that Gallager had on a new suit of clothes. He said: "Gallager, you had better give me those clothes; you will never need them any more." He said it just as though he was not going to be hung, too. Then some one asked Helm if he wanted anything before he died. He asked for a drink and when a glass of whiskey was handed to him, he raised it and said: "Hurrah! for Jeff D——," just then the box was kicked from under him. Helm was a southern man and every time he gave a toast or anything pleased him, he would always cheer for Jeff Davis.

When Mrs. Slade heard that her husband was captured, she left Mountain Meadow with Nailer Thompson, a great friend of Slade's, and hurried to Helena. They rode horseback all day and night, and just as Slade was on the box with the noose around his neck, she came dashing down the mountain on a dead run, her horse covered with foam and in places the foam had frozen. She ran up to the mob and without stopping her horse she leaped down with two drawn revolvers and run into the crowd. Some one took the guns and led her away.. Thompson tried to interfere, but was told to be careful or he would swing, too. As soon as Mrs. Slade was taken away the box was kicked from under her husband.

The rest of the road agents escaped to Deer Lodge. A short time after this the stage running through the Rattlesnake country was held up and Bummer Dan, who had always been a tramp, but had got a sudden raise, was robbed of nine thousand dollars. A young vigilante followed one of the robbers over into Idaho and got the drop on him. The vigilante took advantage of the robber's surprise and used a little strategem. In some way he made the robber believe he had help hidden near by, when there was not a person for miles around. He got the robber to put up his hands, and he tied them together; then he got him on a mule and led the mule under a tree, put one end of a rope around the robber's neck, the other end over a branch of the tree, and told the mule to "Get up." The vigilante left the once desperate road agent a hanging carcass.

I stayed in Montana four months, and during that time sixty-four bandits were hung.

Smith, Holmes, Ritterhouse, Bullock and myself formed a party to go from Helena to Salt Lake. Holmes and Ritterhouse had been freighters from Ogden and sold their cattle and outfit to Darce and Vivian for about twelve thousand dollars, and the rest of us had several thousand between us. We were always on the lookout for the road agents, and wanted to be on the safe side, so we put the money in a pack on some mules and two men were always mounted on good horses to guard the mules, while one did the cooking and watched the wagons. We made a rule for none of us to shoot unless as a signal that the road agents were near.

One night, shortly after we made camp, I strayed away from the others, and suddenly I saw something that caused me to shoot in a hurry. The others came running and awfully excited. I showed them what I had killed, and their excitement changed from fear into keen appetite. I had shot two mountain trout, the two together weighing nineteen pounds.

At Salt Lake City Smith and I left the others and took the road down the Echo canon and headed for Denver. We met some immigrants on the way who warned us of Indians, as there had been a rumor of an uprising. We got across the North Platte before we heard anything more of them, but we were at Marie Anna Station, and well sheltered.

We got into Denver just as the report of the Hungate massacre got there. I immediately joined in with the rescuing and scouting party.

CHAPTER XXXIV.

A TRIP TO THE MISSOURI RIVER.

As Told by A. K. Shaw.

A man by the name of Pease and I happened to run across each other, while on our way to the Missouri river. We were freighting and had several wagons and a large number of oxen with us. On the main traveled side of the river the grass was poor, so we forded the river and made camp on the opposite side.

Right after we had turned the cattle out to graze, we noticed a large and dark cloud coming up over the horizon. We gave the boys orders to prepare a corral, by chaining all the wagons together in a circle, while we gathered up the oxen. Just before we got them to the corral, the storm struck us and the cattle stampeded. Pease and I followed them all that night. Fourteen head got down in a gutter and were stamped to death by the others running over them.

We failed to get them turned back that night, so in the morning we went back to camp for something to eat and to get a new start. The ground was covered with snow and the boys we had left in camp had got up and scraped the snow off a small place so they could build a fire, made some coffee and went back to bed and that is where we found them about noon, when we drifted into camp. We went after the cattle again, but there were sixteen head that we could not find, and we were unable to spend much time in looking. While hunting we were on a sharp lookout for Indians, for there were plenty around us. As I was looking over the country through my field glasses, I saw an object and had Pease to look at it. We both decided that it was an Indian and started after it. As we drew nearer we were sure it was one. When within firing distance, I shot several shots at it, but it did not offer to return the shots or to run. I went still closer and shot again, with the same results. I finally concluded that it was fooling me and was working a scheme. I thought possibly it had something under its robe that prevented the bullets from striking it, and there might be come others hidden in the brush, who would spring out on me when I got near enough.

At last I screwed up courage and took my two revolvers, remounted my horse, and went on a dead run towards it, emptying both revolvers right on to it as I went. Yet it just stood and never offered to fight. When within about twenty feet, I saw that it was not an Indian. Some one had killed a buffalo and cut the meat out, leaving the head and horns on the hide. The meat side had been turned up to the sun and the heat drew it together; then we figured out that the wind must have blowed it up on end and the horns stuck in the sand and the dirt had packed around them, thus holding the hide erect, and at a distance it appeared like an Indian holding his buffalo robe around him.

We took what cattle we had found and went back to camp, rigged up teams enough to take our loads on to the Missouri river.

On the return of our second trip we passed the Malalie ranch, and one of our boys noticed eight head of oxen in their corral, that looked like the ones we had lost on the first trip.

I went in and saw that they were my cattle and asked Malalie about them. He said they were not mine, for they did not have my brand on, and that the commanding officer at Julesburg gave him permission to take in and dispose of all stray stock on the range around his place.

I told him that was all right and I was willing to pay him for the feed and trouble they had cost him, but he would not make any terms, so I went on and made camp a short distance from his place. That evening I took my men and some whiskey and went to call on the Malalies. I treated them all to a drink or two and spent a few sociable minutes; then I went to the corral. The cattle were in a sod corral and it had big strong gates fastened with padlocks. I told Malalie that I was going to take my cattle home, and proceeded to break the lock, opened the gate and ordered the boys to drive the cattle out, while I stood the Malalie bunch off. I had the advantage over them; all my boys were armed, and the others thinking all was friendly and peaceable, had gone out of the house to see us start for home and did not get to their guns before we had ours leveled and saying: "If you make a move we will shoot." We took the cattle on home without any more trouble, but when we got into Julesburg we were arrested and Malalie appeared against us with the complaint that we were stealing his cattle.

They thought they had the cinch on me, for my brand was not on the cattle. Malalie offered to let me go without being prosecuted if I would turn over the cattle and some money to buy him off. I refused and showed them a K on the horns and hoofs of the oxen and also explained how the Malalie brand was made out of my brand, K, on the side. Then I had turned the tables and told him if he would pay me a hundred dollars for damage done to my goods on account of the delay, I would take my cattle off his hands and go on without troubling him any more. He was willing to get rid of me, and since he had made a little off my other eight head he had sold, he consented to let me go on my own terms.

CHAPTER XXXV.

A BUFFALO HUNT.

As Told by John Patterson.

Some of the old residents will remember Jim Kimsey. He was from Southern Illinois, therefore did not know much about fighting Indians before he came to Colorado. But one thing he soon learned was, that he was afraid of them. He said: "Nobody as knows 'em can help being 'fraid of 'em; white folks are hard enough to fight, but Indians are worse, 'cause a fellow keeps thinking what they would do to ye when they gets a chance." He was out after Indians once with Jim Pinkerton and Sam Ashcraft. He said: "I am a good shot at an antelope; can bring them down every time; but I had five fair shots at an old Indian's back, a big, broad-shouldered fellow, too, I'd judge weighed two hundred pounds, but I never made no impression on him."

I have been out with Jim a number of times, and, as he says, he is a good shot. We were out together once on Beaver creek. The whole country was black with buffalo; there seemed to be thousands of them moving north. The Indians had received a permit from the governor of the state to go to Beaver Creek to hunt buffalo. Ouray, Douglas and Colorow, who were Ute Indians, and their band, with Curtis, their interpreter, arrived at the creek in the evening and had a big pow-wow that night. The next morning they said they would show us how to hunt buffalo. They started out in groups of four, two bucks and two squaws, on their ponies. There was a ridge perhaps a quarter of a mile from camp. We went up on that to watch them. The two bucks made a run for the herd and cut out the one they wanted; then one would fire at it, and if he missed the other would fire. As soon as the buffalo was killed the bucks would ride back to camp and the squaws would take charge. They would skin it, cut up the meat and pack it on their ponies and take it into camp.

The Sioux, Cheyennes and Arapahoes claimed this hunting ground, but they camped about thirty-five or forty miles from there. The Utes found out where they were camped and made a raid on them, stole their ponies and struck out for the mountains. The others got on the trail of the Utes and followed them. When they overtook the Utes there was quite a fight and they got their ponies back and some of the Utes' ponies. But the government had to interfere and get back the Ute ponies, because the governor gave them permission to hunt on the grounds belonging to the Sioux, Cheyennes and Arapahoes.

That was the good old time to hunt in Colorado. I brought home twenty-six hind quarters from yearlings up to four-year-olds. My brother, R. Patterson, had twenty-seven hind quarters, and Kimsey had twenty-six. I hung mine up in a sod house and we had buffalo meat all winter, also antelope meat by the wholesale. While we were down there old Chief Douglas came to me and wanted me to give him oats for his horse. He said: "My horse 'Merican horse; no stand ridin' 'out oats." I said: "My horse is American horse, too, and can't stand to pull this load of buffalo back home without oats, and I have only enough for one." So I would not give any.

After we had started home and were about six miles from camp, we met two Englishmen from Greeley, going after a load of buffalo. They had small guns, wholly unfit for such hunting, and the

Indians had got in their wagon and stole their grub, so we gave them something to eat. They then wanted us to kill them a load, but some of the boys in our crowd thought we ought to have a little fun with them first.

They shot one buffalo and just crippled it, then told the men they did not want to waste any more ammunition, but for one of them to go for him with a knife, as it did not have any horns. The calf got the best of them and knocked them down. The boys then called out, "Tail him." "Cut his ham strings," etc. The men went for the calf again, but were knocked down the second time. The boys thought they had fun enough, so they killed some buffalo to load their wagon and sent them on their way rejoicing. We always had good times when we were out, but I think this was our last buffalo hunt.

CHAPTER XXXVI.

MY FIRST INTRODUCTION TO COLORADO.

As Told by Mrs. John Patterson.

In 1866 Colorado was rather a dreary looking place, especially in Weld county, near where the town of Greeley is now located.

Leaving Coultersville, Illinois, the last day of April, in company with Mr. Isaiah Lemon and family, consisting of his two sons and two daughters, we arrived at the mouth of the Poudre on the fifteenth day of July, being eleven weeks on the road. We could hear of Indians before us and back of us; we passed places where there had been ranches burned just a short time before us. I think we saw only two Indians, and they looked as though they had been out on a hunt. We also saw a company of Pawnee soldiers. But we know that it was our Heavenly Father that guided us and kept us from harm.

Uncle Carrol Moore and Aunt Eliza had lived on the banks of the Poudre for several years. They were aunt and uncle to all the people around. The ranchmen just milked cows and cut the native hay for a living. Inside of four years we only heard two sermons, but we started a Sabbath school and did the best we could. One woman remarked that she did not know that any religion had ever crossed the Missouri river; but she found out different.

Uncle Carrol and Aunt Eliza always got along real well with the Indians, who often came down the creek for the squaws to gather prickly pears. They would use wooden tongs to pick the pears to prevent pricking their hands on the thorns. It is said that at one time, in 1864, Fremont saved the lives of his men by this same prickly fruit.

Uncle Carrol said that many times he had seen some of the Indians watching him. He knew they were calculating how would be the best way to kill him.

Uncle said: "I always had my old Spencer ready and they knew what I could do, and that I would shoot if necessary." The Indians never got him. He died some years later in Greeley.

We did have several Indian scares the next year. I would be so frightened that I would not allow any

OX-YOKE AND CHAIN—ACROSS PLAINS, 1864

one to talk of Indians, especially after dark. The alarm would come sometimes when we were preparing to go to bed. The words would be, "All to one house." Then we would have to hustle out and go. We always went to Mrs. Wylie's sod house. We were few in number, but we always made the best of it.

Mrs. Wylie's youngest son and daughter, Sam and Dellia, are still living on the old place. The old sod house was torn down a number of years ago, but the old site is marked by the ox yoke and log chain that Sam Wylie's folks used in crossing the plains from Illinois in 1864.

I think the last big Indian scare was in 1878, in the what was then Weld county. The old Weld county is not near so large now, several counties having been taken off. Quite a number of people had to gather a few goods, get their families in wagons and take them to places of safety.

I understood that Mrs. B. D. Harper was the only woman that remained on a ranch. Three hired men were murdered on the Tracy ranch and the other ranchmen were fired upon. The three murdered men were buried at what is now Sterling. It is stated that the cemetery at Sterling was started at that time. People used to say in early days that out west they had to kill a man to start a cemetery. There is a great change in our fair state since those Indian excitements.

CHAPTER XXXVII.

THE ADVENT OF THE UNION PACIFIC RAILROAD IN THE SUMMER AND FALL OF 1867.

By W. S. Coburn.

In July, 1867, the railroad was completed to Julesburg on the north side of the Platte river from old Julesburg or Fort Sedgwick; thus destroying the business of all overland feed ranches for the coming winter, when all the freighting would be done from Cheyenne, a new town to be surveyed and platted early in August. We at once closed out our surplus stock and abandoned the old fort and ranch, where we had spent several years and had all our experiences with the Indians that we cared for, and went to Julesburg. There we found a new element with the advent of the railroad, consisting of gamblers, thieves, murderers, hold-ups and lewd women, all of whom were in high spirits and doing a thriving business. The town soon had two to three thousand inhabitants, comprising ranchmen like myself, contractors, railroad men, merchants, hotel and saloon men, besides the former referred to. All these, mostly strangers to each other, formed a conglomerate mass of humanity that is seldom seen anywhere except in a new town on the frontier.

They formed a local town government, elected a board of councilmen, police justice, whose name was Hall, and city marshal. They also erected a log jail. We did not know at that time whether we were in Colorado, Nebraska or Wyoming, and as for that it made but very little difference, as the old police justice exclaimed with considerable emphasis, bringing his fist down on the table when a prisoner said he would take an appeal: "Sir, there is no appeal from this court." Many amusing things took place, one of which I will relate: The marshal had six prisoners in the log jail on all kinds of charges from stealing to murder. The jail was located on the next lot from where I was stopping. While the guests were eating dinner one day the prisoners were making a great noise, singing and holloing, and some of the guests at the table made the remark that the prisoners must feel very happy. All this noise was for a purpose, however; some of their friends had furnished the prisoners with a saw and revolvers and they were making this noise to drown the noise of the saw while sawing a log out of the side of the jail so they might escape. When dinner was over I walked out to the front porch and as I was lighting a cigar, the six prisoners came around the corner of the hotel, each with two revolvers, yelling and shooting as they came. They soon found the marshal and disarmed him and compelled him to accompany them to all of the saloons and dance halls and drink with them. Thus they held the town for three hours, when they scattered and took to the sand hills. The old police justice in the meantime had worked himself up to a high pitch, frequently slipping out of his office to get a drink, when the prisoners were down town, until he had about all he could carry. When the prisoners turned the marshal free, he made straight for Judge Hall's office to report what had happened, just as though the judge was not familiar with everything that had gone on. The judge asked the marshal if he knew of any old pioneers that were well armed and mounted on good horses. He told him the three ranchmen from up the river had recently come in, meaning John Fuel, Harvey Blonck and myself. He ordered the marshal to bring us before him at once. When the marshal found us and told us that our immediate presence was wanted, we were at a loss to know what was wanted, and the other two men asked me to be spokesman. When the marshal reported to the judge with us, he was fully "three sheets in the wind," as the sailor would say, and very much excited. He asked about our horses and our arms and when we assured him there was no better armed or mounted men in the territory, he told us that the prisoners had sawed a log out of the jail and escaped. When we told him we were aware of that fact fully three hours ago, he ordered us to mount our horses and go out into the sand hills and capture them, dead or alive. I asked him how we were to know them, telling that hunters for antelopes, which were very plentiful, were out in the hills from town all of the time, and according to his description the prisoners were desperate men, and we would take no chances if we went after them; the first man we saw we would ride to within gunshot and dismount and throw our guns across the saddle and bring him down, then tie him onto a horse and bring him in, to see if he was one of the party wanted. In a new western town it was all excitement and everybody was a stranger to each other. It was a hazardous undertaking and besides, I told the judge that we were preparing to leave the next morning for the new town of Cheyenne, and taking everything into consideration, that we would not go out after his prisoners. One whom the judge was very anxious to capture, went by the name of "Shorty," who he claimed had killed a man a few nights before. We left the judge swearing like a sailor and emphasizing his wrath by pounding his fists on the table and threatening us with dire vengeance.

The next morning we started for a journey of one hundred and sixty miles on our horses for Cheyenne. At noon we stopped at the first ranch, twenty-two miles up Pole creek from Julesburg, and got our dinner, and then sat down in the shade of a sod house to smoke and rest awhile.

While sitting there we saw a lone man about a mile away, coming toward the ranch. It was a very unusual thing to see a man out alone when the country was full of hostile Indians. He kept on coming until he got where we were and took a seat in the shade next to me and asked us which way we were traveling. When we told him we were going to Cheyenne, he asked where we were from, and I told him from Julesburg. He then wanted to know what the news was. I told him there was not much news excepting the prisoners in the jail broke loose the day before and shot up the town and skipped out. I then told him our experiences with the judge and how anxious he seemed to be to capture one of the prisoners, whom, he claimed, had killed a man for money a few nights before, who went by the name of "Shorty." After telling him the whole story, which was very amusing to him, he told me he was the man "Shorty" referred to. After being very much surprised at his announcement, I advised him he had better not go back to Julesburg, or they would hang him as sure as fate. He informed me that he did not intend to go back, but was on his way to Cheyenne, stopping along the route at grading camps at night.

When Cheyenne got started and the track was finished that far in November, 1867, work on the grade was nearly all suspended for the winter, except in the deep cuts in the Black Hills and some rock work. This filled the town with all of the rough element, as well as contractors, graders and a large force of repair men.

I built one of the first buildings in Cheyenne of concrete, 22x80 feet, which stands on Seventeenth street, and was used as a wagon and blacksmith shop a year ago. I also dug the first well on this lot.

When the winter closed in "Shorty" and his band were in full control, stealing horses and running them into the open forks of the mountains, holding up men in the streets in midday and shooting up the town at will. Their headquarters was a saloon by that name in Cheyenne, kept by Dad Cunningham, who was the captain of the band of seventeen men. They usually located in a camp or town one hundred to two hundred miles ahead of where the Union Pacific railroad was completed. During one year there were twenty-six men out of the gang that were hung and shot, and still they kept recruiting, and had seventeen at the finishing of the railroad at Promontory Point on the tenth day of May, 1869.

I was selling goods all along the Union Pacific until it was completed and was personally acquainted with the most of the band of robbers, hold-ups and thieves, but the act of my first introduction by old Judge Hall of Julesburg and meeting one of the principals and relating my experience to him caused me never to be bothered by the gang.

CHAPTER XXXVIII.

GOLD MINERS FROM MONTANA RETURNING TO THE STATES AFTER A SUCCESSFUL TRIP.

In the fall of 1865, twenty-five miners from Alder Gulch, Montana, came down the Platte river on the overland trail, returning to their homes in the states, with a pack train. The least amount of gold dust any one of them had was sixty pounds, and some of them had as much as two hundred pounds; and when one stops to think that four pounds makes approximately one thousand dollars when coined, we can see that they were pretty well fixed. They were well armed with two revolvers and rifles, besides each carried a big hunting knife. They camped on the bank of the Platte river, near my place, one night, and during the night the Indians set fire to the dry grass and made an attempt to kill the men and capture the horses and camp. They were not surprised, however, as they kept a guard out every night. After a pitched battle they succeeded in making their way to my large sod corral. The Indians then gave it up and left, after capturing three fine horses belonging to me, which were tied to a wagon just inside of one of my stables, where I had spread my blankets and was sleeping within thirty feet of my horses and never woke up until the miners were all inside.

There was a man by the name of Black, who had a contract to put up fifteen hundred tons of hay for the government at Julesburg or Fort Sedgwick at one hundred dollars per ton, and the government furnished a company of soldiers to keep the Indians off while he filled the contract.

The Indians cared very little for the regular soldiers and took great delight in decoying them away after two or three Indians, while the balance raided the haymakers, each one of whom carried two revolvers in his belt and a repeating rifle swung to his back. When the men concentrated for self-protection, the Indians would amuse themselves by burning the hay and shooting the men off the mowing machines and capturing the horses. Mr. Black had been so much annoyed by these depredations that he was very much discouraged, and in conversation with the writer a few days before the miners came along, he told him that unless he could get men to protect him he would have to throw up the contract. In the morning I told the miners how the Indians were continually making raids and what Mr. Black had told me a few days previous. After consulting together they said if he would make it an inducement and pay them enough they would guarantee to keep the Indians off while he filled his contract. They at once saw Mr. Black and closed a contract with him for two hundred and fifty dollars per day or ten dollars each. One of their number was appointed cook and the others kept twelve men in the saddle on six-hour shifts night and day. When the Indians came in sight they would all mount their horses and raise a yell and go after them. The Indians soon found that they were not fooling with regular soldiers, and Mr. Black went on and filled his contract, and for the forty days these miners were employed he paid them ten thousand dollars, which added to their already nice stake of gold dust from Montana. They then resumed their journey to the states and their homes, and I never heard of them afterwards.

N. S. HURD

CHAPTER XXXIX.

LOYALTY OF THE PIONEERS.

The hardships undergone by the pioneers and the unfaltering courage with which they faced their trials, have been described to you, not as fully as they might be, for it is impossible to put down in black and white or to find words to express the reality of those early days, so we will let that subject drop and turn to another important and visible factor in the lives of the pioneers, not only in the early days, but now among the few remaining ones.

'Tis a tie that binds them, not as the sworn ties of secret organizations, etc., but a tie of memory and sympathy for their comrades whom fate smiles unkindly upon, and a tie of rejoicing with the more fortunate ones. Circumstances never altered the tie of loyalty that so bound these sturdy and true companions who stood by each other in days of youth and strife up to the days of old age, and let us hope days of rest and comfort, that they so greatly deserve.

To make more clear the loyalty of the pioneers, the address of Hon. N. S. Hurd, who was the president of the Pioneer Society in 1907, and who underwent all the horrors of frontier life and came through them safe and sound, can tell in his own words to a clearer understanding than his already been described.

The following address was given at the expiration of his term as president of the Pioneer Society:

"In vacating the position that I have occupied for the last year as president of the Colorado Pioneer Society, I find that it is hard for me to find language to express to you the gratitude I feel towards you in conferring upon me the privilege of representing you. To be president of this society I consider one of the greatest honors that could be conferred upon any citizen of this state.

There is no gift I could have appreciated more and I wish I had it in my power to more fully express my gratitude, but I can only thank you, while I extend to you my kindest wishes.

We are all growing old together; the ambitions of our lives have been attained or we will have to lay them away among the broken hopes that were incident to the hardships and privations that we had to struggle through when we first came to this country. You remember when we crossed the Missouri river and were leaving civilization six hundred miles in our rear, and like Grant at Vicksburg, our crackerline was cut off and we had severed our connection with the outside world.

What we had to face, we did not know and we cared just a little bit less; we were ready for anything that might come up and we did not care how soon it came up or how long it was deferred; we were always there "with the goods." With the motley throng that crossed the river with us were statesmen, scholars, poets and sages and others that walked in the more humble industries of life; brave men and women that were too brave; in fact, all the cosmopolitan conditions of the whole world were scattered out on the broad American desert. Each one had his own hopes and mighty few fears; we were all upon a common level and we each of us had a 'Howdy' for every one we met upon the trail.

Those were good old days! Many hardships we had to encounter, but then we thought we knew all we had to do was to get on to the banks of Cherry Creek and from its glittering sands of gold take what we wanted, fill our buckskin sacks that we had provided before we left Omaha, and get back to our sweetheart girls early in the fall.

Well, there were very few of us that went back and I am not among the number.

In the meantime I found that I had crossed "Disable" Creek. I had lost my bag and I did not have the wherewithal to buy a postage stamp to write back to my sweetheart girl to tell her how things stood out in this country. And I want to say to you right now that I, like thousands of others, was up against the "real thing."

By this time the grub we had brought from the states was all gone, and I only just have to call your attention to the fact that about that time we were long on appetites.

And here the struggle commenced. The gold sack we had brought from Omaha had long since been forgotten; Cherry Creek had proven an iridescent dream. Its golden sands were as mythical as the fountain of youth for which Ponce de Leon and his brave band prospected this country five hundred years before.

It would be beyond the screen of human vision—no language could convey to one that sees this country now, with all its marvelous beauty and grandeur, how forbidding and desolate it was when you and I first looked upon it, and its unproductive general appearance was just what its name implied, "the Great American Desert."

But we were here and were too brave to go back.

There was just money enough made in big chunks by the lucky ones to make us believe that some day we might get through the cap-rock—that we might be the fortunate ones; but as the days and years went by everything seemed to go from bad to worse and I do not believe I would quite like to tell the epicures of today just how many of us wintered the first few years we were in this country, but the longer we were here, the more faith we had in the final outcome.

But we were building better than we knew.

Each one of us took up some line of industry and the conditions of this country made them all new and untried. Mine was mining and milling, and when I started my mill on Spanish Bar, our amalgamating table was a wooden affair, about eighteen inches wide, with a quicksilver riffle at the lower edge; and if our ore had been fifty per cent gold we could not have saved ten per cent of its value.

And so it was with every industry that now marks the boundaries of this state, which probably has richer and more varied industries than any other country in the world.

As far as my researches have been able to determine, David Wall raised the first vegetables that were grown here. Judge Downing sowed the first seeds of alfalfa, which changed and revolutionized the agricultural condition throughout the whole state. The Marshall coal land was the first one opened for commercial purposes.

It is estimated that we have more coal in Colorado than they have in Pennsylvania. Last year we mined 11,000,000 tons. Pennsylvania mined 183,-000,000. The vast increased condition of commercial enterprises will soon demand that we mine as much coal here as they do there, and when that time comes there will be something doing in the state that you have done so much for. W. H. James, of pleasant memory, and your humble servant set up and ran the first power drill ever operated in Colorado—a ponderous machine on a frame as big as one of the old horse cars that were once so familiar. It took ten men to move it up to the heading of the tunnel; it took from half to three-quarters of an hour to clamp it into place so that it could be operated; and with its immense drill on either side, it looked like one of Uncle Sam's war vessels. Now two men take up a little power drill, pack it anywhere, set it up while you wait, and can do more work with it than we could with the old machine of ancient memory. An old pioneer negro from Joplin, Missouri, built the first smelter and produced the first bullion ever taken out in Colorado, and if he had lived until the present time he might have been at the head of the smelter trust and had great political honors conferred upon him.

It would be interesting to take each one of the many industries that now make our state so great, from their first beginning, at the hands of the old boys, and follow them down through the many changes of their perfections of the present day.

But with all the great glory that has come to our state at your hands, what about the old pioneer? And now I am getting into deep water. The theme is too large; the responsibility in trying to do justice to them is too great for my ability.

I look over this little handful of old gray-haired veterans before me here tonight, and memory is busy in its backward flight, and it conjures up the forms and faces of those who are not here—companions of our lives who stood beside us when the storm of adversity gathered around and the future held out but little hope; then their smiles were the brightest and they cheered us on to better efforts and nobler deeds—good wives—God bless them! But they sleep their last long sleep.

But we mourn for our dead, and, like Rachel, we fail to be comforted. But listen! We think we can almost hear the stroke of the silent oarsman as he comes across the dark river to gather in the remnant of our little band, and soon we will be on the other shore where the 'Ho, Jo,' of the miner may be sounded in a brighter and better land than this.

The full honor and glory of the pioneer will not come while you and I live, but with song and story, and with marble shafts, the memory of your lives will be perpetuated by coming generations. The brightest pages of history will be those that contain the names and deeds of those who carved an empire out of this forbidden land.

We drop a silent tear; we hear the dull thud of the earth as it falls upon the grave of one of our number; we have performed the last duty to one that has been with us so long.

Another pioneer is gone. And right here let me say that the first pioneer that was buried by our society was a man whose financial condition when I first knew him, was as sound as that of any man in the state.

Thousands of cattle and wagons between here and the river were his, the fortunes of war and the vicissitudes of life turned hard against him and our good old friend, Judge Steck, assisted him through bankruptcy, where the liabilities were $862,000, and when he was buried by our society, he did not have a single cent. Let us stay close together, my boys, for we cannot tell what the whirligig of time may do to us.

His or her place can never be filled. Pioneers cannot be made and some one in the days that are not far distant will be the last of the Mohicans. And while we pay tribute to the dead, our first duty is to the living. It has been our hope in days that have passed that some of our big hearted, wealthy members would donate to our society a suitable home where our declining years could be passed, surrounded by the comforts that old age requires. This may never be, but I think I know the feeling of the people of Denver and Colorado well enough to know that no pioneer shall ever want for the necessities of life, and let this be our duty to one another.

While I am no longer your president, I am still a pioneer, and any time I can be of service to the 'old boys' individually or collectively, I will be ready to do what I can. Our strenuous work is over and what we want now is social enjoyment and all the comforts that there is in life. My hope is that this may be yours. And may peace be with you."

CHAPTER XL.

CONCLUSION.

These few short stories were told to the writer by three pioneers who took an active part in the early settlement of Colorado.

It has been their desire for several years past to make known to the public (and especially to the citizens of the state of Colorado who have reaped the benefits of the labor, hardships and endurance of the pioneers), the suffering, fear and toils that so barred the settlement in the early days.

Being a Colorado girl and wanting the foundation builders of her native state to get credit for the work they did, the writer undertook to write these stories as they were told to her.

Kind readers, compare the West as it was fifty years ago when the white men first began to settle in it, to what it is today.

Is it any wonder that Colorado has risen up among the leading states of the union?

When it had so sturdy and brave builders, it took not only strength and endurance of body, but mind and determination as well, to undergo their struggles and face the dangers and discouragements they met with, and yet keep pushing their way forward, never wavering or turning back.

There were times when it seemed as though they were working in the dark, and could not see their way through, and often tempted with the question, "Will we accomplish anything or is this just a waste of time?"

In those darkest days, the fearless frontiersmen would urge onward, giving a helping hand to each other, all working together for one object, "the development of the West."

The unselfish consideration for each other was plainly marked throughout the years on the frontier by the settlers. They thought nothing of time or money if their neighbors were in need. They thought nothing of self or fear if any one was in danger. They never asked gold or silver for their services. They knew if need be they would have the same aid and protection that had been rendered to their neighbor. One common characteristic of these frontiersmen is, they are modest about their valor, and when asked about their part of early-day struggles and achievements, they try to put you off with, "Oh, I did nothing extra." Upon a great deal of urging and questioning you can bring to light many deeds that one would almost imagine to be impossible; privations and suffering that would seem beyoud endurance. Yet these pioneers did nothing, to let them tell it, but down in their hearts they know they did. Can anything stand without a foundation? Does not the strength and lasting qualities of any accomplishment depend upon what it is built of? If the frontiersmen had said "fail" and given up, this West would not have been the enterprising land that it is today.

If it had been people weak in body and mind that had started westward first, the savages would have conquered them and this would remain a half-civilized country instead of growing to the advancement of civilization that it has reached in such few years.

There were a great many other battles and struggles that are not spoken of in this book, yet they did their part toward opening the gateway into the West and making a garden of prosperity and progress out of the once barren wilderness.

The success of the pioneers proves that "Effort is never in vain"—a lesson for the present generation to follow. Cultivate the determination and endurance of the forefathers and carry on the work they began. "Push onward with the standard of civilization and turn the wheels of progress until our West has reached the last round of advancement and development."

www.ingramcontent.com/pod-product-compliance
Lightning Source LLC
Chambersburg PA
CBHW070532160426
43199CB00014B/2249